YouTube for Beginners: How to Start & Grow Your YouTube Channel

Roy Hendershot

Published by Roy Hendershot, 2024.

YOUTUBE FOR BEGINNERS: HOW TO START & GROW YOUR YOUTUBE CHANNEL

First edition. June 26, 2024.

Copyright © 2024 Roy Hendershot.

Written by Roy Hendershot.

Table of Contents

Chapter 1: Introduction to YouTube

YouTube has transformed the way we consume media, offering a platform where anyone can share their creativity, knowledge, and passions with the world. Since its inception, YouTube has grown exponentially, becoming a significant force in the digital age. This book aims to guide you through starting and growing your own YouTube channel, even if you're a complete beginner.

Understanding YouTube's vast audience is crucial. With billions of users worldwide, YouTube offers a diverse viewership interested in nearly every topic imaginable. This diversity is a goldmine for creators who can find and engage with niche audiences. The key is to identify what makes you unique and how you can share that with others.

Creating a personal brand on YouTube is more than just a hobby; it's an opportunity to build a community and even a career. Many YouTubers have turned their channels into full-time jobs, thanks to the platform's monetization options. However, success doesn't happen overnight. It requires dedication, creativity, and a willingness to learn and adapt.

One of the most exciting aspects of starting a YouTube channel is the potential for growth and earnings. YouTube's monetization options, such as ad revenue, sponsorships, and merchandise, provide numerous ways to turn your passion into profit. However, building a successful channel takes time, effort, and a clear strategy.

To kickstart your YouTube journey, it's essential to set realistic goals. What do you want to achieve with your channel? Whether it's to share your hobbies, educate others, or build a brand, having clear objectives will guide your content creation process. Start small and celebrate every milestone you reach.

The YouTube algorithm plays a significant role in how your content is discovered. Understanding how it works can help you optimize your videos for better visibility. The algorithm favors videos with high engagement, including likes, comments, and watch time. Therefore, creating engaging content that resonates with your audience is crucial.

Consistency is another critical factor in YouTube success. Regular uploads help keep your audience engaged and signal to YouTube that you're an active creator. Develop a content schedule that works for you and stick to it. Whether you upload weekly, bi-weekly, or monthly, consistency builds trust with your audience.

Analytics and metrics are your best friends on YouTube. They provide insights into how your videos are performing and how viewers are interacting with your content. Use this data to refine your strategies, identify what's working, and make necessary adjustments. Tools like YouTube Studio offer a wealth of information to help you grow.

Patience and perseverance are essential qualities for any YouTuber. Building a successful channel takes time, and there will be challenges along the way. However, each obstacle is an opportunity to learn and improve. Stay motivated, keep experimenting with new ideas, and never be afraid to make mistakes.

Engaging with your community is vital for growth. Respond to comments, ask for feedback, and create content that addresses your viewers' interests and questions. Building a loyal community not only boosts your channel's engagement but also creates a supportive network that encourages your continued growth.

As you embark on your YouTube journey, remember that creativity is your most valuable asset. Don't be afraid to think outside the box and try new things. The most successful YouTubers are those who bring something unique to the platform and aren't afraid to take risks.

Building a personal brand on YouTube involves more than just creating videos. It's about sharing your personality, values, and passions in a way that resonates with others. Your brand should be authentic and reflect who you are. This authenticity will attract viewers who share your interests and values.

Legal considerations are also important when starting a YouTube channel. Ensure you have the rights to use any music, images, or clips in your videos. Familiarize yourself with YouTube's community guidelines to avoid any potential issues that could result in strikes or account suspension.

Understanding the YouTube algorithm is crucial for maximizing your reach. The algorithm prioritizes videos that retain viewers and generate engagement. Focus on creating high-quality content that keeps viewers watching until the end and encourages them to interact through likes, comments, and shares.

Success on YouTube is measured in various ways. While subscriber count and views are important, engagement metrics like watch time, likes, and comments are equally crucial. These metrics provide a more accurate picture of how well your content resonates with your audience.

Patience is key when growing your channel. It's rare for a channel to become an overnight success. Consistent effort, a willingness to learn, and adapting to feedback are essential components of long-term growth. Celebrate small victories and stay focused on your goals.

The YouTube community is incredibly supportive. Engage with other creators, join online forums, and participate in events. Networking with other YouTubers can lead to collaborations, new ideas, and valuable feedback. Building relationships within the community enriches your experience and opens up new opportunities.

Staying motivated can be challenging, especially when progress seems slow. Find inspiration in your passion for your content and the impact you're making on your viewers. Take breaks when needed to recharge your creativity and avoid burnout.

Leveraging other social media platforms can help grow your YouTube channel. Share your videos on Instagram, Twitter, Facebook, and other platforms where your target audience is active. Cross-promotion increases your reach and drives traffic to your YouTube channel.

Successful YouTubers often share similar traits: creativity, resilience, and a genuine passion for their content. Studying their journeys can provide valuable insights and inspiration. Learn from their successes and failures to refine your own strategies.

Reflecting on the reasons why you want to start a YouTube channel helps clarify your goals and motivations. Whether it's sharing your knowledge, connecting with others, or creating a new career path, understanding your 'why' will drive your efforts and keep you focused.

Chapter 2: Why Start a YouTube Channel?

———

Starting a YouTube channel offers numerous personal and professional benefits. One of the most compelling reasons is the opportunity to share your passions and interests with a global audience. Whether you're passionate about cooking, gaming, beauty, or education, YouTube provides a platform to showcase your expertise and connect with like-minded individuals.

Building a community around your interests is incredibly rewarding. As you share your content, you'll attract viewers who share your passions. Over time, these viewers become a loyal audience who engage with your videos, provide feedback, and support your growth. This sense of community is one of the most fulfilling aspects of being a YouTuber.

The potential for financial gain is another significant motivation for starting a YouTube channel. Through ad revenue, sponsorships, merchandise sales, and other monetization options, many YouTubers turn their channels into lucrative businesses. While making money shouldn't be the sole reason for starting a channel, it's a realistic and achievable goal with dedication and effort.

Developing new skills is a natural part of the YouTube journey. From video production and editing to marketing and branding, creating content for YouTube involves a wide range of skills that can enhance your personal and professional life. These skills are not only valuable for your channel but can also be applied to other areas of your career.

Enhancing your personal brand is a powerful benefit of having a YouTube channel. By consistently sharing high-quality content, you establish yourself as an authority in your niche. This can lead to speaking engagements, collaborations, and other opportunities that further your professional development.

Networking opportunities are abundant on YouTube. Connecting with other creators in your niche opens the door to collaborations, knowledge sharing, and mutual support. These relationships can be incredibly valuable, providing new perspectives and opportunities for growth.

The joy of creative expression is perhaps the most satisfying reason to start a YouTube channel. Whether you're passionate about storytelling, educating, or entertaining, YouTube offers a platform to unleash your creativity and share it with the world. The process of creating and sharing content is immensely fulfilling and provides a creative outlet.

Documenting your journey and progress is another compelling reason to start a YouTube channel. Whether you're documenting a fitness journey, a travel adventure, or a personal project, YouTube allows you to capture and share your experiences with a global audience. This documentation not only serves as a personal archive but also inspires and motivates others.

Educating and inspiring others is a powerful motivator for many YouTubers. Sharing your knowledge and experiences can have a significant impact on your viewers' lives. Whether you're teaching a new skill, providing valuable insights, or offering inspiration, your content can make a difference and leave a lasting impact.

The power of storytelling on YouTube is immense. Through compelling narratives and relatable experiences, you can connect with your audience on a deeper level. Stories have the ability to engage, inspire, and motivate viewers, making them a valuable tool in your content creation arsenal.

Creating a portfolio of work is another benefit of starting a YouTube channel. Your videos serve as a showcase of your skills, creativity, and expertise. This portfolio can be valuable for future opportunities, whether you're seeking freelance work, collaborations, or career advancements.

Expanding your reach and influence is a natural outcome of growing a YouTube channel. As your audience grows, so does your ability to impact and influence others. This expanded reach opens up new opportunities for collaborations, sponsorships, and other ventures.

Opportunities for collaboration are abundant on YouTube. Working with other creators can lead to new ideas, expanded audiences, and valuable partnerships. Collaboration not only benefits your channel but also enriches your content and provides fresh perspectives.

Turning hobbies into a career is a dream for many people, and YouTube makes this possible. Whether you're passionate about gaming, cooking, or beauty, creating content around your hobbies can lead to a fulfilling and profitable career. The journey from hobbyist to professional is challenging but immensely rewarding.

Understanding the YouTube culture is essential for success on the platform. YouTube has its own set of norms, trends, and community dynamics. Immersing yourself in this culture helps you create content that resonates with your audience and stays relevant.

The democratization of media through YouTube is one of its most significant impacts. Unlike traditional media, YouTube allows anyone with a camera and an internet connection to share their content with the world. This democratization empowers creators and provides a platform for diverse voices and perspectives.

Becoming a thought leader in your field is a powerful outcome of building a successful YouTube channel. By consistently sharing valuable insights and expertise, you position yourself as an authority in your niche. This thought leadership can lead to speaking engagements, consulting opportunities, and other professional advancements.

The flexibility and freedom of being a YouTuber are unparalleled. Unlike traditional jobs, being a YouTuber allows you to set your own schedule, work from anywhere, and pursue your passions. This flexibility is a significant advantage, providing a better work-life balance and greater personal fulfillment.

The impact of visual content in communication cannot be overstated. Videos are a powerful medium for conveying information, emotions, and stories. As a YouTuber, you harness this power to create content that engages and inspires your audience.

Using YouTube as a marketing tool is another benefit of starting a channel. Whether you're promoting a business, a product, or a personal brand, YouTube provides a platform to reach a broad and engaged audience. Effective use of video marketing can significantly boost your visibility and success.

Creating a legacy through your content is a profound motivator for many YouTubers. Your videos are a lasting testament to your creativity, knowledge, and impact. They have the potential to inspire and educate future generations, leaving a lasting legacy.

The therapeutic aspect of content creation is often overlooked but highly valuable. Sharing your experiences, thoughts, and emotions through video can be a form of self-expression and emotional release. Many YouTubers find that creating content is a way to process and reflect on their lives.

As you prepare to start your YouTube channel, remember that the journey is as important as the destination. Enjoy the process of creating, learning, and connecting with others. The rewards of being a YouTuber go beyond financial gain, offering personal growth, fulfillment, and the joy of sharing your passions with the world.

Chapter 3: What to Make Videos About

————

Identifying your passions and interests is the first step in deciding what to make videos about. Think about what excites you, what you enjoy talking about, and what you can share with others. Your passion will shine through in your videos, making them more engaging and authentic.

Researching popular content in your niche can provide valuable insights into what works and what doesn't. Look at successful channels in your area of interest and analyze their content. What topics do they cover? How do they engage their audience? Use this research to inform your content strategy while adding your unique twist.

Balancing personal interest with audience demand is crucial for success on YouTube. While it's important to create content you're passionate about, it's equally important to consider what your audience wants to see. Find a balance that allows you to stay true to yourself while catering to viewer interests.

Experimenting with different types of content is a great way to find what works best for you and your audience. Try out various formats such as tutorials, vlogs, reviews, and interviews. Pay attention to which types of videos perform well and resonate with your viewers.

Analyzing your competitors can provide valuable insights and inspiration. Look at what other creators in your niche are doing and identify gaps or opportunities that you can capitalize on. However, avoid copying them outright; instead, use their content as a springboard for your unique ideas.

Finding your unique voice and style is essential for standing out on YouTube. Think about what makes you different from other creators and how you can bring that uniqueness into your content. Your personality, storytelling, and perspective are what will attract and retain viewers.

Authenticity is key to building a loyal audience. Be yourself and let your personality shine through in your videos. Viewers appreciate genuine, relatable content and are more likely to engage with and support creators who are authentic.

There are countless content ideas for various niches. For educational channels, consider creating how-to videos, tutorials, and informative content. Lifestyle channels can feature vlogs, day-in-the-life videos, and personal stories. Think about what aligns with your interests and expertise.

Educational and how-to videos are highly popular on YouTube. These videos provide value to viewers by teaching them new skills or knowledge. If you have expertise in a particular area, consider creating educational content that helps others learn and grow.

Vlogs and lifestyle content offer a glimpse into your daily life and experiences. These videos are more personal and help viewers connect with you on a deeper level. Share your adventures, routines, and personal stories to create a relatable and engaging channel.

Showcasing your skills and talents is another great content idea. Whether you're an artist, musician, chef, or athlete, share your talents with the world. Demonstrate your skills, share tips and tricks, and inspire others to pursue their passions.

Content planning and brainstorming techniques can help you generate a steady stream of video ideas. Keep a running list of ideas and use mind maps to explore different topics. Regularly set aside time to brainstorm and plan your content calendar.

Engaging your audience with interactive content can boost engagement and viewer retention. Consider creating Q&A videos, challenges, and live streams where viewers can interact with you directly. This not only makes your content more engaging but also strengthens your community.

Storytelling is a powerful tool for engaging viewers. Incorporate narratives and personal stories into your videos to make them more compelling. Whether you're sharing a personal experience or telling a fictional story, storytelling can captivate your audience and keep them coming back for more.

Creating series and episodic content can keep viewers engaged and coming back for more. Consider developing a series around a specific topic or theme. This not only provides structure to your content but also encourages viewers to watch multiple videos.

Leveraging trends and challenges can help boost your channel's visibility. Stay updated on current trends and popular challenges within your niche and create relevant content. Participating in trends shows that your channel is active and engaged with the YouTube community.

Collaborating with other YouTubers is a great way to expand your reach and bring fresh ideas to your channel. Partner with creators who share similar interests or have complementary audiences. Collaborations introduce your channel to new viewers and provide valuable networking opportunities.

Using audience feedback for content ideas is highly effective. Pay attention to the comments and messages from your viewers. They can provide valuable insights into what they enjoy and what they want to see more of. Use this feedback to shape your content strategy.

Balancing evergreen content with timely topics is essential for maintaining a relevant and engaging channel. Evergreen content, such as tutorials and how-to videos, remains relevant over time and continues to attract views. Timely topics, such as current events or trends, can provide short-term boosts in visibility.

The role of humor and entertainment in your videos can't be overstated. Even educational or serious content can benefit from a touch of humor and entertainment. Incorporate your personality and sense of humor to make your videos enjoyable and engaging.

Creating inspirational and motivational content can have a profound impact on your viewers. Share your personal journey, challenges, and successes to inspire and motivate others. This type of content resonates deeply with viewers and fosters a loyal and supportive community.

Documenting your personal journey is another compelling content idea. Whether you're on a fitness journey, learning a new skill, or working on a personal project, share your progress with your audience. This not only provides valuable content but also creates a sense of accountability and motivation.

Incorporating different formats, such as tutorials, reviews, and vlogs, keeps your content diverse and interesting. Experiment with various formats to see what resonates with your audience. This diversity also keeps your content fresh and engaging.

Content diversity is essential for keeping your audience engaged. While it's important to have a consistent theme, varying your content format and topics can prevent viewer fatigue. Explore different angles and approaches to your niche to keep things interesting.

Final tips for choosing your content focus include staying true to your passions, listening to your audience, and continuously experimenting with new ideas. Remember, the most successful YouTube channels are those that balance personal interest with audience demand, authenticity with innovation, and creativity with strategy.

Chapter 4: Overcoming the Fear of Getting Started

Starting a YouTube channel can be intimidating, especially if you're not used to being in front of the camera. Common fears include judgment, criticism, and the pressure to be perfect. However, it's important to remember that every successful YouTuber started somewhere and faced similar challenges.

Dealing with the fear of judgment and criticism is a significant hurdle for many new creators. It's natural to worry about what others will think, but it's important to focus on your passion and purpose. Remember, not everyone will appreciate your content, and that's okay. Focus on those who do and use their support to stay motivated.

Building confidence in front of the camera takes practice. Start by recording yourself in a relaxed setting, talking about topics you're passionate about. The more you practice, the more comfortable you'll become. Don't be afraid to watch your recordings and critique yourself constructively. This self-review helps you improve and build confidence.

Overcoming perfectionism is crucial for getting started on YouTube. It's easy to get caught up in the desire to create perfect content, but this can be paralyzing. Understand that your first videos won't be perfect, and that's okay. Focus on progress rather than perfection. Each video you make is an opportunity to learn and improve.

Setting small, achievable goals can help you overcome the fear of getting started. Instead of aiming for perfection, set realistic goals that you can accomplish. For example, aim to upload your first video, regardless of its quality. Celebrate each milestone, no matter how small, as it brings you closer to your overall goal.

Embracing mistakes and learning from them is a vital part of the YouTube journey. Every successful YouTuber has made mistakes along the way. View these mistakes as learning opportunities rather than failures. The more you learn and adapt, the better your content will become.

Seeking support from friends and family can provide a confidence boost. Share your goals with those close to you and ask for their encouragement and feedback. Having a support system can make the process less daunting and more enjoyable.

Using positive self-talk and affirmations can help combat negative thoughts and boost your confidence. Remind yourself of your strengths, accomplishments, and the reasons why you're starting your YouTube channel. Positive affirmations can help shift your mindset and reduce anxiety.

Preparing mentally for public scrutiny is important. Understand that being a public figure, even on a small scale, comes with exposure to public opinion. Focus on your passion and purpose, and remember that not all feedback is personal. Learn to filter constructive criticism from negativity.

Everyone starts somewhere, and it's important to remember that the journey to success is a process. The most successful YouTubers didn't achieve overnight fame; they worked hard, learned from their mistakes, and stayed committed to their goals. Be patient with yourself and enjoy the learning process.

Developing a growth mindset is essential for overcoming fear. A growth mindset focuses on learning and improvement rather than fixed abilities. Embrace challenges as opportunities to grow and view setbacks as part of the journey. This mindset shift can reduce fear and increase resilience.

Focusing on progress rather than perfection can help you stay motivated. Celebrate each step forward, no matter how small. Each video you create, each new subscriber, and each positive comment is a sign of progress. By focusing on growth, you'll stay motivated and less intimidated by the process.

Finding motivation in your 'why' can help you overcome fear. Remind yourself why you started your YouTube channel. Whether it's to share your passion, educate others, or build a community, keeping your 'why' in mind can drive you forward, even when you feel discouraged.

Setting up a comfortable filming environment can reduce anxiety. Choose a quiet, well-lit space where you feel at ease. Having a dedicated filming area can help you get into the right mindset and reduce distractions.

Techniques for reducing camera anxiety include deep breathing, visualization, and practice. Before filming, take a few deep breaths to calm your nerves. Visualize yourself speaking confidently and engaging with your audience. The more you practice, the more natural it will feel.

The role of preparation in building confidence cannot be overstated. Plan your videos in advance, create an outline or script, and rehearse your talking points. The more prepared you are, the more confident you'll feel when the camera starts rolling.

Recording practice videos is a great way to build confidence. These videos don't have to be perfect or even published. Use them as a way to get comfortable with the camera, test your equipment, and refine your delivery. Over time, you'll notice improvement and feel more confident.

Watching and learning from other creators can provide inspiration and tips for overcoming fear. Observe how they present themselves, handle mistakes, and engage with their audience. Learning from others can boost your confidence and provide new ideas for your content.

Using constructive criticism to improve is essential. Not all feedback will be positive, but constructive criticism can be incredibly valuable. Use it to identify areas for improvement and refine your content. Remember, feedback is an opportunity to grow.

Celebrating small victories along the way can keep you motivated. Whether it's your first video upload, your first subscriber, or positive feedback from a viewer, each milestone is worth celebrating. These small victories remind you of your progress and keep you focused on your goals.

Self-care and balance are crucial for maintaining motivation and reducing anxiety. Take breaks when needed, prioritize your well-being, and avoid burnout. A healthy balance between work and relaxation ensures that you stay motivated and enjoy the process.

Turning fear into excitement is a powerful mindset shift. Instead of viewing the fear of starting as a negative, reframe it as excitement for the new opportunities and experiences ahead. This positive perspective can reduce anxiety and increase motivation.

Finally, remember that the journey is a learning experience. Every video you create, every challenge you face, and every success you achieve is part of your growth as a YouTuber. Embrace the process, stay persistent, and enjoy the ride. The fear of getting started will diminish over time, and your confidence will grow with each step you take.

Chapter 5: Starting Your New Channel

Starting your new YouTube channel is an exciting step in your journey as a creator. The first step is setting up your YouTube account. If you don't already have a Google account, you'll need to create one. Once you have your Google account, you can easily set up your YouTube channel and start customizing it.

Choosing a name for your channel is an important decision. Your channel name should reflect your content and be memorable to your audience. Consider using keywords related to your niche to make it easier for viewers to find your channel. Your name is your brand, so take your time to choose something that represents you well.

Crafting a compelling channel description is the next step. Your channel description should provide an overview of what viewers can expect from your content. Include relevant keywords to improve your channel's discoverability. Be clear, concise, and engaging to attract potential subscribers.

Designing your channel's visual identity is crucial for making a strong first impression. Create a custom channel banner that reflects your brand and adds a professional touch to your channel. Use high-quality images and graphics to make your banner visually appealing. Consistency in your visuals helps build your brand identity.

Setting up your profile picture is another important aspect of your channel's visual identity. Choose a clear, high-quality image that represents you or your brand. Your profile picture appears next to your comments and videos, so make sure it's recognizable and professional.

Writing a strong 'About' section helps viewers understand what your channel is about. Use this space to introduce yourself, explain your content, and highlight what makes your channel unique. Include links to your social media profiles and website to connect with your audience on other platforms.

Adding links and social media handles to your channel helps viewers find you on other platforms. You can add links to your website, social media profiles, and other relevant sites. This not only increases your online presence but also provides additional ways for viewers to engage with you.

Organizing your channel layout makes it easier for viewers to navigate your content. Use sections and playlists to categorize your videos and create a user-friendly experience. Highlight your most popular videos, recent uploads, and content series to guide viewers through your channel.

Setting up playlists and categories helps keep your content organized. Playlists group related videos together, making it easier for viewers to find and watch multiple videos on the same topic. Categorizing your content also improves your channel's SEO and discoverability.

The importance of a consistent upload schedule cannot be overstated. Regular uploads keep your audience engaged and signal to YouTube that you're an active creator. Develop a content schedule that works for you and stick to it. Consistency builds trust with your audience and helps you grow your channel.

Planning your first set of videos is an exciting step. Think about what topics will resonate with your audience and showcase your expertise. Create a content calendar to plan your uploads and ensure you have a steady stream of videos ready to go. Preparation is key to maintaining a consistent upload schedule.

Preparing for your channel launch involves more than just creating videos. Consider how you'll promote your channel and engage with your audience. Use social media, email newsletters, and collaborations to spread the word and attract viewers. A successful launch sets the stage for long-term growth.

Strategies for promoting your new channel include leveraging your existing networks, engaging with online communities, and using SEO techniques. Share your videos on social media, participate in forums related to your niche, and use relevant keywords in your titles and descriptions. Promotion is essential for building an audience.

Engaging with your audience from the start helps build a loyal community. Respond to comments, ask for feedback, and create content that addresses your viewers' interests and questions. Engagement boosts your channel's visibility and fosters a supportive network of viewers.

The role of trailers and introductory videos is crucial for attracting new subscribers. Create a channel trailer that introduces your content and highlights what viewers can expect. Keep it short, engaging, and informative. A well-crafted trailer can convert casual viewers into loyal subscribers.

Setting expectations for your viewers is important for building trust. Be clear about your upload schedule, the type of content you create, and what viewers can expect from your channel. Consistent communication helps manage expectations and fosters a positive viewer experience.

Learning from your first few uploads is essential for improvement. Analyze the performance of your initial videos, gather feedback, and make necessary adjustments. Pay attention to what resonates with your audience and refine your content strategy accordingly.

Analyzing early feedback and metrics provides valuable insights. Use YouTube Studio to track your video performance, engagement, and audience demographics. This data helps you understand what's working and what needs improvement. Regular analysis is key to optimizing your content and growing your channel.

Adjusting your content strategy as needed ensures that you stay relevant and engaging. Based on feedback and performance metrics, tweak your content to better meet the needs of your audience. Flexibility and adaptability are crucial for long-term success on YouTube.

Building momentum with regular uploads keeps your audience engaged and helps you grow. As you establish a consistent upload schedule, you'll see increased viewer retention and engagement. Regular uploads signal to YouTube that you're an active creator, boosting your channel's visibility.

The importance of patience and persistence cannot be overstated. Building a successful YouTube channel takes time and effort. There will be challenges and setbacks, but persistence and a positive mindset will keep you moving forward. Celebrate your progress, no matter how small, and stay focused on your goals.

Networking with other new creators can provide valuable support and inspiration. Join online communities, participate in forums, and connect with other YouTubers in your niche. Collaboration and mutual support can accelerate your growth and enhance your content.

Leveraging community features on YouTube, such as comments, polls, and live streams, helps build a strong connection with your audience. Use these features to engage with your viewers, gather feedback, and create a sense of community. Active engagement fosters loyalty and boosts your channel's visibility.

Final tips for a successful channel launch include staying true to your passion, being consistent, and engaging with your audience. Enjoy the process, celebrate your progress, and stay committed to your goals. With dedication and effort, your YouTube channel will grow and thrive.

Chapter 6: Create Your YouTube Account

————

Creating your YouTube account is the first step to starting your channel. Begin by setting up a Google account if you don't already have one. This Google account will be used to access YouTube and all its features. Once you have your Google account, go to YouTube and sign in.

Navigating the YouTube interface is straightforward. After signing in, click on your profile picture in the top right corner and select "Create a Channel." You'll be prompted to enter your channel name and choose a category. This is the start of building your online presence.

Choosing between a personal or brand account is an important decision. A personal account is linked to your Google account and uses your name, while a brand account allows you to use a business or brand name. Brand accounts also enable multiple users to manage the channel, which is useful if you plan to collaborate with others.

Setting up your YouTube settings is the next step. Go to YouTube Studio, where you can customize your channel settings, upload defaults, and community settings. This includes setting your channel's privacy, adding managers, and configuring advanced features like monetization and branding.

Verifying your account for advanced features is essential for accessing additional YouTube tools. Verification allows you to upload longer videos, add custom thumbnails, and live stream. To verify your account, go to YouTube's verification page and follow the instructions to receive a verification code via phone.

Linking your social media accounts helps expand your online presence. You can add links to your social media profiles, website, and other relevant sites in your channel's About section. This makes it easier for viewers to find and connect with you across different platforms.

Setting up monetization options is an exciting part of creating your channel. Once your channel meets YouTube's eligibility criteria, you can apply for the YouTube Partner Program. This allows you to earn revenue from ads, channel memberships, and merchandise. Monetization provides an incentive to create high-quality content consistently.

Understanding YouTube's community guidelines is crucial for maintaining a positive channel environment. Familiarize yourself with the guidelines to avoid content strikes and potential account suspension. YouTube's community guidelines cover topics like hate speech, harassment, and copyright infringement.

Exploring YouTube Studio is essential for managing your channel. YouTube Studio provides tools for uploading videos, analyzing performance, and engaging with your audience. Use the dashboard to track your channel's analytics, respond to comments, and manage your video content.

Setting up your channel's default settings can save you time. Go to the Upload defaults section in YouTube Studio and configure settings like video privacy, category, and tags. These defaults will apply to all future uploads, streamlining the upload process.

The importance of two-factor authentication cannot be overstated. Enabling two-factor authentication adds an extra layer of security to your account. This protects your channel from unauthorized access and potential hacking attempts. Go to your Google account settings to enable this feature.

Managing your channel's privacy settings is crucial for controlling who can see your content. You can choose to make your videos public, private, or unlisted. Public videos are visible to everyone, private videos are only accessible to you, and unlisted videos can be shared via a direct link.

Customizing your notification preferences helps you stay updated on your channel's activity. You can choose to receive notifications for comments, mentions, and other interactions. This ensures you stay engaged with your audience and respond promptly to their feedback.

Adding managers or collaborators to your account is useful if you're working with a team. Brand accounts allow you to add multiple managers who can access and manage the channel. This is particularly helpful for larger projects or collaborations with other creators.

Setting up your channel's watermark adds a professional touch to your videos. Watermarks are small logos or images that appear in the corner of your videos, reinforcing your brand identity. Go to YouTube Studio and navigate to the Branding section to upload your watermark.

Creating a custom URL for your channel makes it easier for viewers to find and remember your channel. Once your channel meets YouTube's eligibility criteria, you can create a custom URL that reflects your brand name. This is a valuable branding tool that enhances your online presence.

Using YouTube's help and support resources is beneficial for new creators. YouTube provides extensive resources, including tutorials, forums, and support articles, to help you navigate the platform. Take advantage of these resources to learn best practices and troubleshoot any issues you encounter.

Common account setup mistakes to avoid include using copyrighted content without permission, neglecting security measures, and ignoring community guidelines. Being aware of these pitfalls can help you set up a successful and compliant YouTube channel.

Updating your account information regularly ensures that your channel remains relevant and secure. Keep your contact information, channel description, and social media links up to date. Regular updates reflect your active engagement and commitment to your channel.

Protecting your account from hacks is essential for maintaining your channel's security. Use strong passwords, enable two-factor authentication, and be cautious of phishing attempts. Regularly monitor your account for any suspicious activity and take immediate action if you notice anything unusual.

Exploring YouTube's additional features can enhance your content creation experience. YouTube offers various tools and features, such as live streaming,

YouTube Shorts, and community posts, to engage with your audience in different ways. Experiment with these features to diversify your content.

Keeping your account information secure is a top priority. Regularly review your security settings, update your passwords, and enable all available security features. A secure account ensures the safety of your content and your audience's trust.

Final tips for a successful account setup include staying organized, regularly updating your settings, and leveraging YouTube's resources. Enjoy the process of building your channel, and remember that each step brings you closer to your goals. With a well-set-up account, you're ready to start creating and sharing your content with the world.

Chapter 7: Choose Your Channel's Visuals

Choosing your channel's visuals is a vital step in creating a memorable and professional YouTube presence. Your visuals include your channel logo, banner, thumbnails, and overall design elements that reflect your brand identity. These visuals play a crucial role in attracting and retaining viewers.

Designing a memorable channel logo is the first step. Your logo should be simple, recognizable, and reflective of your brand. Consider using a professional graphic designer or logo creation tools to develop a high-quality logo. A strong logo helps establish your brand identity and makes your channel easily identifiable.

Creating an eye-catching channel banner is equally important. Your banner is the first thing viewers see when they visit your channel, so make it visually appealing and informative. Include your channel name, tagline, and upload schedule if possible. Use high-quality images and graphics to make your banner stand out.

Choosing a consistent color scheme helps reinforce your brand identity. Select a palette of colors that complement each other and use them consistently across your channel's visuals. Consistency in colors creates a cohesive look and makes your channel more professional and recognizable.

Selecting fonts that reflect your brand is another important consideration. Choose fonts that are easy to read and match the tone of your content. Use these fonts consistently in your thumbnails, banners, and video graphics to maintain a uniform look.

Using high-quality images and graphics is essential for creating professional visuals. Invest in good quality photos, graphics, and design elements to enhance your channel's appearance. High-quality visuals not only look better but also convey a sense of professionalism and attention to detail.

Creating thumbnails that stand out is crucial for attracting viewers. Thumbnails are like mini-advertisements for your videos, so make them engaging and eye-catching. Use bold colors, clear images, and concise text to capture viewers' attention. A well-designed thumbnail can significantly increase your click-through rate.

Designing a channel intro and outro adds a professional touch to your videos. An intro is a short clip that introduces your channel and sets the tone for your content, while an outro wraps up your video and encourages viewers to subscribe or watch more videos. Consistent intros and outros enhance your brand identity and provide a polished look to your videos.

Using visual storytelling in your videos can make them more engaging and impactful. Incorporate visuals that support and enhance your narrative. Whether it's through graphics, animations, or B-roll footage, visual storytelling helps convey your message more effectively.

Branding plays a significant role in viewer retention. Consistent and professional visuals create a strong brand identity that viewers recognize and trust. A well-branded channel encourages viewers to subscribe, return for more content, and recommend your channel to others.

There are many tools and software available for graphic design. Programs like Adobe Photoshop, Canva, and PicMonkey offer a range of features for creating professional visuals. Invest time in learning these tools to enhance your design skills and create high-quality visuals for your channel.

Working with designers and freelancers can be beneficial if you're not confident in your design skills. Platforms like Fiverr and Upwork connect you with talented designers who can create custom visuals for your channel. Collaborating with professionals ensures that your visuals are top-notch and align with your brand.

The impact of visuals on your channel's success cannot be overstated. High-quality and consistent visuals attract viewers, enhance your brand identity, and contribute to a professional and polished look. Investing in good visuals is essential for standing out on YouTube.

Balancing creativity with consistency is key to maintaining a strong visual identity. While it's important to be creative and innovative, ensure that your visuals remain consistent with your brand. Consistency builds recognition and trust with your audience.

Incorporating your personality into your visuals makes your channel more relatable and engaging. Use colors, fonts, and images that reflect your style and personality. Personal touches in your visuals help viewers connect with you on a deeper level.

Updating your visuals as your channel evolves is important for staying relevant. As your brand grows and changes, your visuals should reflect these updates. Regularly review and refresh your visuals to keep them aligned with your brand's current identity.

The role of animations and effects in your videos can enhance viewer engagement. Use animations and visual effects to emphasize key points, add humor, or create a dynamic viewing experience. However, use them sparingly to avoid overwhelming your audience.

Creating a cohesive look across all platforms ensures that your brand is easily recognizable. Use the same visuals and design elements on your YouTube channel, social media profiles, and website. Consistency across platforms strengthens your brand identity and makes it easier for viewers to find and follow you.

Using templates and presets can streamline your design process. Many graphic design tools offer templates and presets for banners, thumbnails, and other visuals. These resources save time and ensure that your visuals are professional and consistent.

The importance of visual accessibility cannot be overlooked. Ensure that your visuals are accessible to all viewers, including those with visual impairments. Use high-contrast colors, readable fonts, and descriptive text for images. Accessibility enhances the viewing experience for all audiences.

Testing different visual styles can help you find what resonates best with your audience. Experiment with various colors, fonts, and designs to see what works. Use YouTube analytics to track the performance of your visuals and make data-driven decisions.

Analyzing the visuals of successful channels in your niche provides valuable insights. Look at how top creators design their banners, thumbnails, and other visuals. Learn from their strategies and apply similar techniques to your own channel while adding your unique touch.

Collecting feedback on your visuals helps you improve. Ask your audience for their opinions on your thumbnails, banners, and other design elements. Use this feedback to make adjustments and enhance your visual identity.

Keeping up with design trends ensures that your visuals remain fresh and modern. Follow design blogs, participate in online communities, and stay updated on the latest trends in graphic design. Incorporate relevant trends into your visuals while maintaining your brand's unique identity.

Final tips for perfecting your channel's visuals include staying true to your brand, using high-quality design elements, and consistently updating your visuals. Enjoy the process of creating and refining your visual identity. With strong visuals, your YouTube channel will attract and retain viewers, helping you grow and succeed.

Chapter 8: Beat Perfectionism

———

Perfectionism can be a significant barrier to starting and growing a YouTube channel. Understanding the roots of perfectionism is the first step in overcoming it. Perfectionism often stems from a fear of failure or judgment. Recognizing these underlying fears can help you address and manage them.

The negative impacts of perfectionism on creativity are profound. Striving for perfection can stifle your creativity and prevent you from taking risks. Embracing imperfection allows you to explore new ideas, experiment with different formats, and ultimately create more authentic and engaging content.

Setting realistic expectations for yourself is crucial. Understand that your first videos won't be perfect, and that's okay. Focus on progress rather than perfection. Set achievable goals that push you to improve without overwhelming you. Celebrate each milestone, no matter how small.

Embracing imperfection and authenticity can make your content more relatable. Viewers appreciate genuine, imperfect content that reflects real life. Instead of striving for perfection, aim to create content that is honest and true to your personality. Authenticity builds trust and fosters a loyal audience.

The importance of taking action cannot be overstated. Perfectionism often leads to procrastination, as the fear of not being perfect prevents you from starting. Taking action, even if it's imperfect, is better than not starting at all. Each step you take brings you closer to your goals.

Strategies for overcoming perfectionist tendencies include setting deadlines, focusing on progress, and practicing self-compassion. Set specific deadlines for your videos to prevent endless tweaking. Focus on the progress you're making rather than the end result. Be kind to yourself and recognize that everyone makes mistakes.

Focusing on progress over perfection helps you stay motivated. Celebrate each step forward, no matter how small. Each video you create, each new subscriber, and each positive comment is a sign of progress. By focusing on growth, you'll stay motivated and less intimidated by the process.

Learning to accept constructive criticism is essential. Not all feedback will be positive, but constructive criticism can be incredibly valuable. Use it to identify areas for improvement and refine your content. Remember, feedback is an opportunity to grow and not a reflection of your worth.

Setting achievable goals and deadlines can help you overcome perfectionism. Instead of aiming for flawless content, set realistic goals that you can accomplish. For example, aim to upload your first video, regardless of its quality. Celebrate each milestone, no matter how small, as it brings you closer to your overall goal.

The role of self-compassion in content creation is vital. Be kind to yourself and recognize that everyone makes mistakes. Treat yourself with the same understanding and patience you would offer to a friend. Self-compassion reduces the pressure to be perfect and encourages a healthier approach to content creation.

Celebrating your successes and milestones can keep you motivated. Whether it's your first video upload, your first subscriber, or positive feedback from a viewer, each milestone is worth celebrating. These small victories remind you of your progress and keep you focused on your goals.

Understanding that mistakes are part of learning is essential. Every successful YouTuber has made mistakes along the way. View these mistakes as learning opportunities rather than failures. The more you learn and adapt, the better your content will become.

Seeking inspiration from other creators can provide motivation and new ideas. Observe how they present themselves, handle mistakes, and engage with their audience. Learning from others can boost your confidence and provide new perspectives on your content.

Practicing mindfulness and stress reduction techniques can help manage perfectionism. Techniques such as deep breathing, meditation, and visualization can reduce anxiety and help you stay focused. Incorporate these practices into your routine to maintain a healthy mindset.

Avoiding comparisons with others is crucial. It's easy to compare yourself to more established creators and feel inadequate. Remember that everyone's journey is different. Focus on your progress and celebrate your unique strengths and achievements.

The benefits of a growth mindset cannot be overstated. A growth mindset focuses on learning and improvement rather than fixed abilities. Embrace challenges as opportunities to grow and view setbacks as part of the journey. This mindset shift can reduce fear and increase resilience.

Balancing quality with quantity is key to overcoming perfectionism. While quality is important, it's also essential to produce content consistently. Find a balance that allows you to create high-quality videos without getting bogged down in perfectionist tendencies.

Delegating tasks and seeking help can reduce the pressure to be perfect. If possible, collaborate with others or outsource tasks that you find challenging. Delegation allows you to focus on your strengths and ensures that your content is well-rounded and professional.

The importance of regular uploads cannot be overstated. Consistent uploads signal to YouTube that you're an active creator and help build a loyal audience. Regular uploads also provide more opportunities to learn and improve, reducing the pressure to create perfect content.

Accepting that done is better than perfect is a powerful mindset shift. Striving for perfection can lead to endless tweaking and delays. Focus on completing your videos and getting them out to your audience. Each video you publish is an opportunity to learn and improve.

Building a supportive network of peers can provide encouragement and motivation. Connect with other YouTubers who understand the challenges of content creation. Share experiences, offer feedback, and support each other's growth. A supportive network can reduce feelings of isolation and boost your confidence.

Creating a routine that works for you helps manage perfectionism. Establish a workflow that includes time for planning, filming, editing, and reviewing. A structured routine reduces the pressure to be perfect and ensures that you consistently produce content.

Prioritizing tasks and focusing on what matters can reduce perfectionist tendencies. Identify the most important aspects of your content and focus on those. Let go of minor details that don't significantly impact the overall quality of your videos.

Using feedback to improve rather than to criticize yourself is essential. Constructive feedback is a tool for growth, not a reflection of your worth. Use feedback to identify areas for improvement and make necessary adjustments. This approach encourages a healthier and more productive mindset.

Final thoughts on overcoming perfectionism include embracing imperfection, focusing on progress, and practicing self-compassion. Enjoy the process of creating and sharing your content. Remember, the journey is as important as the destination. Each step you take brings you closer to your goals and helps you grow as a creator.

Chapter 9: Brainstorm Video Ideas

Generating a steady stream of video ideas is crucial for maintaining a successful YouTube channel. The importance of consistent content generation cannot be overstated. Regular uploads keep your audience engaged and signal to YouTube that you're an active creator.

Techniques for brainstorming video ideas include keeping a running list of topics, using mind maps, and researching trends in your niche. Whenever inspiration strikes, jot down your ideas in a notebook or digital document. This running list becomes a valuable resource when planning your content calendar.

Using mind maps for content planning helps organize your thoughts and explore different angles. Start with a central topic and branch out into subtopics, related themes, and specific video ideas. Mind maps visually represent your ideas and can spark new connections and insights.

Researching trending topics in your niche provides valuable insights into what's currently popular. Use tools like Google Trends, YouTube's trending page, and social media to identify trends. Creating content around trending topics can boost your channel's visibility and attract new viewers.

Analyzing your competitors' content can provide inspiration and identify gaps in the market. Look at what other creators in your niche are doing and think about how you can offer a unique perspective or add value. Competitor analysis helps you stay competitive and relevant.

Seeking inspiration from your audience is highly effective. Pay attention to the comments and messages from your viewers. They can provide valuable insights into what they enjoy and what they want to see more of. Use this feedback to shape your content strategy.

Leveraging social media for content ideas is another great strategy. Platforms like Twitter, Instagram, and Facebook are rich sources of inspiration. Follow influencers, join relevant groups, and participate in discussions to stay updated on current trends and gather new ideas.

Collaborating with other creators can bring fresh perspectives to your channel. Partner with YouTubers who share similar interests or have complementary audiences. Collaborations introduce your channel to new viewers and provide valuable networking opportunities.

The role of keyword research in content planning is crucial. Use tools like Google Keyword Planner and YouTube's search bar to identify popular search terms related to your niche. Incorporate these keywords into your video titles, descriptions, and tags to improve your discoverability.

Creating a content calendar helps you plan your uploads and ensure you have a steady stream of videos ready to go. A content calendar provides structure and keeps you organized. Plan your videos a month or two in advance to stay consistent and avoid last-minute stress.

Balancing evergreen and trending content is essential for maintaining a relevant and engaging channel. Evergreen content, such as tutorials and how-to videos, remains relevant over time and continues to attract views. Timely topics, such as current events or trends, can provide short-term boosts in visibility.

The importance of variety in your content cannot be overstated. While it's important to have a consistent theme, varying your content format and topics can prevent viewer fatigue. Explore different angles and approaches to your niche to keep things interesting.

Experimenting with different video formats can help you find what resonates best with your audience. Try out various formats such as tutorials, vlogs, reviews, and interviews. Pay attention to which types of videos perform well and refine your content strategy accordingly.

Using analytics to refine your ideas provides valuable insights into what's working and what needs improvement. YouTube Studio offers detailed analytics on video performance, audience demographics, and engagement metrics. Use this data to make informed decisions about your content.

Planning content series and themed months can keep viewers engaged and coming back for more. Develop a series around a specific topic or theme. This not only provides structure to your content but also encourages viewers to watch multiple videos.

Keeping your content aligned with your brand is essential for building a loyal audience. Ensure that your video ideas reflect your brand's values, tone, and personality. Consistent branding helps viewers recognize and trust your content.

Using audience feedback to shape your content strategy is highly effective. Pay attention to what your viewers are saying in the comments and messages. Their feedback provides valuable insights into what they enjoy and what they want to see more of. Use this feedback to refine your content.

Reimagining popular content in your own style can provide new ideas. Look at successful videos in your niche and think about how you can put your unique spin on them. This approach allows you to create relevant content while showcasing your personality and creativity.

Incorporating seasonal and holiday themes into your content can boost engagement. Create videos around holidays, seasons, and special events that resonate with your audience. Seasonal content provides timely and relevant videos that attract viewers.

The role of personal experiences in content creation is significant. Sharing your personal journey, challenges, and successes can make your content more relatable and engaging. Personal stories resonate deeply with viewers and foster a sense of connection.

Staying updated with industry news and trends ensures that your content remains relevant. Follow industry blogs, news sites, and influencers to stay informed about the latest developments in your niche. Incorporate this information into your videos to provide value to your viewers.

Balancing informational and entertainment value is crucial for engaging viewers. While it's important to provide valuable information, adding entertainment elements keeps your videos interesting and enjoyable. Find a balance that works for your content and audience.

Avoiding content burnout through proper planning is essential. Content burnout occurs when you run out of ideas or lose motivation. Regular brainstorming, planning, and taking breaks when needed can prevent burnout and keep you inspired.

Final tips for effective content brainstorming include staying true to your passions, listening to your audience, and continuously experimenting with new ideas. Enjoy the process of creating and sharing your content. With a steady stream of fresh ideas, your YouTube channel will grow and thrive.

Chapter 10: Script Your Video

———

Scripting your videos is a valuable practice that enhances the quality and clarity of your content. The benefits of scripting include providing structure, ensuring you cover all key points, and reducing the likelihood of forgetting important information. A well-written script helps you deliver your message clearly and confidently.

Different approaches to video scripting work for different creators. Some prefer detailed scripts with every word written out, while others use bullet points or outlines to guide their speaking. Find an approach that works for you and allows you to maintain a natural and engaging delivery.

Finding your unique voice and tone is essential for scripting. Your script should reflect your personality and style, making your content more relatable and engaging. Write as you speak to keep your delivery natural and authentic. This approach helps build a connection with your audience.

Structuring your video script is crucial for maintaining viewer engagement. Start with a strong introduction that hooks your viewers and clearly states what the video is about. The body of your script should cover your main points in a logical order, and the conclusion should summarize the key takeaways and encourage viewers to take action.

Writing engaging intros and outros is important for capturing and retaining viewer attention. Your intro should be compelling and set the stage for the rest of the video. The outro should wrap up your content, encourage viewers to like, comment, and subscribe, and provide a call to action for further engagement.

Balancing information and entertainment is key to creating engaging videos. While it's important to provide valuable information, adding entertainment elements keeps your viewers interested. Use humor, storytelling, and visual aids to make your content enjoyable and engaging.

Techniques for writing conversationally include using simple language, avoiding jargon, and writing as you speak. Imagine you're having a conversation with a friend and write in a friendly, approachable tone. This makes your content more relatable and easier to understand.

Using storytelling in your scripts can make your content more engaging. Incorporate personal stories, anecdotes, and examples to illustrate your points. Storytelling not only makes your content more interesting but also helps convey complex information in a relatable way.

The importance of clarity and conciseness cannot be overstated. Keep your scripts clear and to the point, avoiding unnecessary details that can confuse or bore your audience. Focus on delivering your message effectively and concisely to maintain viewer engagement.

Writing for different video formats requires flexibility. Tutorials, reviews, vlogs, and interviews each have unique scripting needs. Adapt your scripting style to suit the format of your video while maintaining your unique voice and tone. This versatility ensures that your content remains engaging and relevant.

Incorporating humor and personality into your scripts makes your videos more enjoyable. Use humor to lighten the mood and make your content more relatable. Let your personality shine through to build a connection with your audience and keep them coming back for more.

Preparing for on-screen spontaneity is important, even with a script. Leave room for ad-libs and natural interactions to keep your delivery lively and authentic. This spontaneity adds a personal touch and makes your videos feel less scripted and more genuine.

Practicing your script before filming helps improve your delivery. Read through your script multiple times, practicing your tone, pacing, and expressions. The more familiar you are with your script, the more confident and natural you'll appear on camera.

Using bullet points and outlines can provide a flexible scripting approach. Instead of writing out every word, use bullet points to highlight key points and guide your speaking. This method allows for a more spontaneous and conversational delivery while ensuring you cover all important information.

Avoiding common scripting mistakes is essential for creating high-quality content. These mistakes include being too rigid, using complex language, and neglecting the audience's perspective. Focus on creating scripts that are clear, engaging, and audience-centered.

Incorporating calls to action in your scripts encourages viewer engagement. Whether it's asking viewers to like, comment, subscribe, or visit a website, calls to action prompt viewers to take the next step. Be clear and concise in your calls to action, and integrate them naturally into your script.

Adapting your script based on feedback helps you improve. Pay attention to viewer comments and feedback, and use this information to refine your scripting style. Regularly reviewing and adjusting your scripts ensures that your content remains relevant and engaging.

The role of ad-libs and improvisation in your scripts adds authenticity. While a script provides structure, leaving room for spontaneous interactions makes your videos feel more natural. Practice balancing scripted content with impromptu moments to enhance your delivery.

Writing scripts for collaboration videos requires coordination and flexibility. Collaborate with your partner to ensure your scripts align and complement each other. Focus on creating a cohesive narrative that highlights each creator's strengths and provides value to both audiences.

Ensuring your script aligns with your visuals is crucial for a cohesive video. Plan your visuals alongside your script to ensure they complement and enhance your content. This alignment creates a seamless viewing experience and makes your videos more engaging.

Reviewing and revising your script is an important step in the scripting process. After writing your initial draft, review it for clarity, conciseness, and engagement. Make necessary revisions to improve your script and ensure it effectively communicates your message.

Using teleprompters and other aids can help with script delivery. Teleprompters allow you to read your script while maintaining eye contact with the camera. This tool is particularly useful for longer or more complex scripts. Practice using a teleprompter to ensure a smooth and natural delivery.

The importance of a strong closing statement cannot be overstated. Your closing statement should summarize the key points of your video, reinforce your call to action, and leave a lasting impression on your viewers. A well-crafted closing statement encourages viewers to engage with your content further.

Collecting feedback on your scripting style helps you improve. Ask your audience for their opinions on your delivery, clarity, and engagement. Use this feedback to make adjustments and refine your scripting process. Regularly seeking feedback ensures that your content continues to resonate with your audience.

Final tips for effective video scripting include finding your unique voice, practicing your delivery, and continuously refining your scripts. Enjoy the process of creating and sharing your content. With well-written scripts, your YouTube videos will be engaging, informative, and memorable.

Chapter 11: Film With Your Phone

———

Filming with your phone is a convenient and accessible way to create high-quality YouTube videos. Modern smartphones have advanced cameras that can produce impressive video quality. The advantages of using a phone for filming include portability, ease of use, and affordability.

Choosing the right phone for video production is the first step. Look for phones with high-resolution cameras, good low-light performance, and features like image stabilization. Popular options include the latest models from Apple, Samsung, and Google. Investing in a good phone ensures that your videos are visually appealing.

Setting up your phone for optimal filming is crucial. Start by cleaning the lens to ensure clear footage. Use the highest resolution and frame rate available on your phone. Explore your camera's settings to adjust exposure, white balance, and focus for the best results. Proper setup enhances the quality of your videos.

Understanding your phone's camera settings can significantly improve your video quality. Learn how to manually adjust settings like exposure, focus, and white balance. Manual control allows you to fine-tune your shots and achieve a professional look. Experiment with different settings to find what works best for your content.

Using external lenses can enhance your phone's camera capabilities. Attachments like wide-angle, macro, and telephoto lenses provide more creative options and improve the overall quality of your footage. These lenses are easy to use and can significantly enhance your video production.

Stabilizing your phone for smooth footage is essential. Use a tripod or a gimbal to keep your phone steady while filming. Handheld shots can be shaky and distract viewers. Stabilization tools ensure that your videos are smooth and professional. They also allow for more creative and dynamic shots.

The importance of good lighting cannot be overstated. Proper lighting enhances the quality of your videos and makes them more visually appealing. Use natural light whenever possible, and supplement with artificial lights if needed. Position your lights to eliminate shadows and highlight your subject effectively.

Recording high-quality audio with your phone is achievable with the right tools. External microphones, such as lavalier or shotgun mics, significantly improve audio quality. Built-in phone microphones often capture background noise and lack clarity. Investing in a good external microphone ensures clear and professional audio.

Using tripods and mounts for steady shots is crucial for professional-looking videos. A stable setup eliminates camera shake and allows for more precise framing. Tripods are versatile and come in various sizes and styles to suit different filming needs. Mounts and grips provide additional stability and control.

Techniques for framing and composition enhance the visual appeal of your videos. Follow the rule of thirds, leading lines, and symmetry to create balanced and engaging shots. Experiment with different angles and perspectives to add variety and interest to your footage. Good composition makes your videos more visually appealing.

Filming in different environments requires adaptability. Adjust your settings and setup based on the location and lighting conditions. Indoor and outdoor environments present unique challenges and opportunities. Be prepared to adapt your filming techniques to achieve the best results in any setting.

Managing storage and battery life is essential for uninterrupted filming. Ensure your phone has enough storage space for your videos, and carry a portable charger or extra batteries. Regularly transfer your footage to a computer or external storage to free up space on your phone. This ensures you're always ready to film.

Editing on your phone versus on a computer has its pros and cons. Mobile editing apps offer convenience and ease of use, while computer software provides more advanced features and flexibility. Choose the option that best suits your workflow and needs. Both methods can produce high-quality edits.

Using apps for editing and enhancing footage can streamline your process. Apps like Adobe Premiere Rush, iMovie, and Kinemaster offer powerful editing tools directly on your phone. These apps allow you to trim, add effects, adjust colors, and export your videos with ease. Mobile editing apps are perfect for quick edits and on-the-go production.

Common mistakes to avoid when filming with a phone include poor lighting, shaky footage, and bad audio. Ensure you have adequate lighting, use stabilization tools, and invest in a good microphone. Avoid filming in noisy or cluttered environments that can distract viewers. Addressing these common issues improves your video quality.

Leveraging your phone's features for creative shots can enhance your content. Explore features like slow motion, time-lapse, and HDR to add variety and interest to your videos. Experiment with different shooting modes and effects to create unique and engaging footage. Your phone's capabilities offer endless creative possibilities.

Filming in different resolutions and frame rates provides flexibility. Higher resolutions like 4K offer stunning clarity, while lower resolutions save storage space. Different frame rates create various effects, from cinematic 24fps to smooth 60fps. Choose the resolution and frame rate that best suit your content and style.

The importance of a good background setup cannot be overstated. Choose a clean, clutter-free background that complements your subject. Use props and decorations to add interest and context to your videos. A well-thought-out background enhances the overall aesthetic of your footage.

Recording in different lighting conditions requires adaptability. Adjust your settings and setup based on the available light. Use reflectors and diffusers to control natural light, and add artificial lights if needed. Proper lighting ensures that your subject is well-lit and your footage is clear and professional.

Using phone accessories for better production quality can enhance your videos. Accessories like external microphones, lenses, tripods, and stabilizers improve audio and visual quality. Investing in these tools ensures that your content is professional and engaging. Accessories also provide more creative options and flexibility.

Tips for filming on the go include using portable equipment, planning your shots in advance, and being adaptable. Travel light and use compact gear that's easy to carry. Plan your filming schedule and locations to maximize efficiency. Stay flexible and ready to adapt to changing conditions.

Capturing dynamic shots and angles adds interest to your videos. Experiment with different perspectives, such as low angles, overhead shots, and moving shots. Dynamic footage keeps viewers engaged and adds a professional touch to your content. Use your phone's mobility to explore creative filming techniques.

Testing and experimenting with your phone helps you understand its capabilities. Try different settings, modes, and accessories to see what works best for your content. Regular testing ensures that you're familiar with your equipment and can achieve the best results. Experimentation fosters creativity and innovation.

Reviewing and improving your filming technique is an ongoing process. After each shoot, review your footage and identify areas for improvement. Focus on refining your composition, lighting, and audio quality. Regularly updating your techniques ensures that your videos remain high-quality and engaging.

Final tips for successful phone filming include investing in good accessories, understanding your phone's features, and practicing regularly. Enjoy the process of creating and experimenting with your phone. With the right techniques and tools, you can produce professional-quality videos that captivate your audience.

Chapter 12: Upgrading Your Camera Setup

Upgrading your camera setup is an exciting step in enhancing your video production quality. While filming with a phone is convenient, upgrading to a dedicated camera offers more control and better image quality. When and why to upgrade your camera setup depends on your goals and needs. If you're looking to improve your video quality, have more creative control, and explore advanced features, upgrading is a worthwhile investment.

Choosing the right camera for your needs involves understanding different types of cameras and their features. DSLRs and mirrorless cameras are popular choices for YouTubers due to their versatility and high image quality. Consider factors like resolution, frame rates, low-light performance, and lens compatibility when selecting a camera. Research and compare different models to find the best fit for your content.

Understanding camera specifications helps you make an informed decision. Key specifications to consider include sensor size, megapixels, ISO range, and autofocus capabilities. Larger sensors, higher megapixels, and better low-light performance contribute to superior image quality. Understanding these specs ensures that you choose a camera that meets your filming needs.

Comparing different types of cameras can help you decide which one suits your style. DSLRs offer excellent image quality and a wide range of lenses, but they can be bulky. Mirrorless cameras are more compact and provide similar quality, making them a popular choice for vloggers. Action cameras like GoPros are great for on-the-go filming and capturing dynamic shots. Each type of camera has its advantages, so choose based on your filming style and needs.

Essential camera accessories enhance your setup and improve your videos. External microphones, tripods, stabilizers, and lighting equipment are crucial for achieving professional-quality footage. Invest in high-quality accessories that complement your camera and suit your filming style. Accessories not only improve your video quality but also provide more creative options.

Setting up your new camera for filming involves configuring the settings for optimal performance. Adjust the resolution, frame rate, and focus settings based on your content needs. Explore your camera's manual settings to fine-tune exposure, white balance, and ISO. Proper setup ensures that your camera performs at its best and produces high-quality footage.

Adjusting camera settings for optimal quality requires understanding manual controls. Manual settings give you more control over your footage, allowing you to adjust exposure, focus, and color balance. Experiment with different settings to achieve the desired look and feel for your videos. Understanding manual controls is essential for professional-quality production.

Using manual versus auto settings depends on your comfort level and filming needs. Manual settings provide more control and flexibility, but auto settings can be convenient for quick shoots. Start with auto settings and gradually transition to manual as you become more comfortable. Balancing both approaches ensures that you're prepared for various filming scenarios.

The importance of lenses in video production cannot be overstated. Different lenses offer unique perspectives and creative options. Wide-angle lenses capture expansive scenes, while telephoto lenses are great for close-ups. Prime lenses offer superior image quality, while zoom lenses provide versatility. Investing in high-quality lenses enhances your camera's capabilities and improves your video quality.

Techniques for shooting with a DSLR or mirrorless camera include understanding depth of field, focus, and exposure. Use shallow depth of field to create a cinematic look with blurred backgrounds. Manual focus allows for precise control, especially in low-light conditions. Adjusting exposure settings ensures that your footage is well-lit and visually appealing. Practice these techniques to master your camera and achieve professional results.

Using external microphones for better audio is crucial for high-quality production. Internal camera microphones often lack clarity and capture background noise. External microphones, such as shotgun or lavalier mics, provide clear and professional audio. Good audio quality is essential for engaging videos, so invest in a reliable microphone.

Stabilizing your camera with gimbals and tripods ensures smooth and steady footage. Handheld shots can be shaky and distract viewers. Gimbals provide motorized stabilization for dynamic shots, while tripods offer stability for static shots. Using stabilization tools enhances the professionalism of your videos and keeps viewers engaged.

Filming in different lighting conditions requires adaptability and proper setup. Use natural light when possible, but supplement with artificial lights in low-light situations. Adjust your camera settings to compensate for changing lighting conditions. Understanding how to work with different lighting scenarios ensures that your footage is consistently high-quality.

Managing storage and file formats is essential for smooth production. High-resolution videos consume significant storage space, so use high-capacity memory cards and external drives. Choose file formats that balance quality and storage efficiency. Regularly back up your footage to avoid data loss and ensure that you're always ready to film.

The role of white balance and color grading in video production is significant. White balance settings ensure that colors are accurate and consistent. Color grading in post-production enhances the visual appeal and sets the mood of your videos. Understanding these techniques helps you create visually stunning content.

Tips for shooting in different environments include adapting your setup and techniques to the location. Indoor and outdoor environments present unique challenges and opportunities. Adjust your camera settings, use appropriate lighting, and consider environmental factors like weather and noise. Being adaptable ensures that you achieve the best results in any setting.

Maintaining and caring for your camera equipment prolongs its lifespan and ensures optimal performance. Regularly clean your lenses, sensor, and body to prevent dust and dirt buildup. Store your equipment in a safe, dry place and use protective gear when traveling. Proper maintenance keeps your gear in top condition and ready for filming.

Troubleshooting common camera issues helps you address problems quickly and efficiently. Issues like blurry footage, poor lighting, and audio problems can be frustrating. Learn basic troubleshooting techniques to resolve these issues on the spot. Being prepared ensures that you can handle any challenges during filming.

Integrating your camera with other equipment enhances your production quality. Use accessories like external monitors, audio recorders, and lighting kits to create a professional setup. Understanding how to connect and use these tools ensures that your footage is high-quality and engaging.

Using camera settings for creative effects adds interest to your videos. Techniques like slow motion, time-lapse, and HDR provide unique visual effects. Experiment with these settings to add variety and creativity to your content. Creative effects enhance viewer engagement and make your videos stand out.

Capturing high-quality B-roll footage enhances your main content. B-roll provides supplementary footage that adds context and visual interest. Use B-roll to cover cuts, illustrate points, and add variety to your videos. High-quality B-roll improves the overall production value of your content.

Shooting time-lapses and slow-motion videos offers creative options. Time-lapses condense long events into short, engaging clips, while slow motion highlights details and adds drama. Experiment with these techniques to create dynamic and visually appealing videos. These effects enhance your storytelling and keep viewers engaged.

The impact of camera angles and movement on your videos is significant. Different angles and movements create visual interest and enhance storytelling. Use techniques like panning, tilting, and tracking to add dynamism to your shots. Experiment with angles to find what best suits your content and style.

Reviewing and improving your camera technique is an ongoing process. After each shoot, review your footage and identify areas for improvement. Focus on refining your composition, lighting, and audio quality. Regularly updating your techniques ensures that your videos remain high-quality and engaging.

Final tips for upgrading your camera setup include investing in quality gear, understanding your camera's features, and practicing regularly. Enjoy the process of learning and experimenting with your new equipment. With the right setup and techniques, you can produce professional-quality videos that captivate your audience.

Chapter 13: Set Up Your Audio

The importance of good audio quality in video production cannot be overstated. Clear and professional audio enhances the viewer experience and makes your content more engaging. Poor audio quality can distract viewers and detract from your message. Investing in good audio equipment and techniques ensures that your videos sound as good as they look.

Choosing the right microphone for your needs is the first step to improving your audio quality. Different types of microphones serve different purposes. Shotgun microphones are great for directional audio, lavalier microphones are ideal for on-the-go recording, and USB microphones are perfect for voiceovers and studio recordings. Select a microphone that suits your filming style and needs.

Setting up external microphones ensures that you capture high-quality audio. External microphones provide better clarity and reduce background noise compared to built-in camera or phone microphones. Use shock mounts and windshields to further enhance audio quality and minimize interference.

Recording audio with your camera or phone requires proper setup and accessories. External microphones connect to your camera or phone via adapters or audio interfaces. Ensure that your microphone is securely connected and positioned correctly for optimal audio capture. Test your audio setup before filming to avoid issues during recording.

Reducing background noise and interference is crucial for clear audio. Choose a quiet filming location and use soundproofing materials like foam panels or blankets to minimize ambient noise. Turn off noisy appliances and avoid filming near busy streets or other sources of background noise.

Techniques for clear and crisp audio include proper microphone placement and speaking techniques. Position your microphone close to your mouth but out of the frame to capture clear audio. Speak clearly and at a consistent volume to ensure that your audio is easy to understand. Practice good diction and avoid mumbling.

Using audio editing software enhances your recorded audio. Programs like Audacity, Adobe Audition, and GarageBand offer tools for noise reduction, equalization, and compression. These tools help you refine your audio and eliminate any imperfections. Learning basic audio editing techniques ensures that your audio is professional and polished.

Syncing audio with video footage is essential for a seamless viewing experience. Use clapperboards or clap your hands at the start of recording to create a sync point. In post-production, align the audio and video tracks using this sync point. Proper synchronization ensures that your audio matches your video perfectly.

Troubleshooting common audio issues helps you address problems quickly and efficiently. Issues like background noise, echo, and distortion can be frustrating. Learn basic troubleshooting techniques to resolve these issues on the spot. Being prepared ensures that you can handle any challenges during filming.

The role of soundproofing in audio quality is significant. Soundproofing materials like foam panels, carpets, and heavy curtains help absorb sound and reduce echo. Create a dedicated recording space with soundproofing to achieve clear and professional audio. Proper soundproofing enhances the overall quality of your recordings.

Using pop filters and windshields minimizes unwanted noise. Pop filters reduce plosive sounds (such as 'p' and 'b' sounds) that can cause distortion, while windshields minimize wind noise during outdoor recording. These accessories are inexpensive but highly effective in improving audio quality.

Recording in different environments requires adaptability. Indoor and outdoor environments present unique audio challenges. Use appropriate microphones and accessories for each setting and adjust your setup based on ambient noise and acoustics. Being adaptable ensures that you achieve the best audio quality in any location.

Balancing audio levels is crucial for clear and consistent sound. Use audio editing software to adjust volume levels and ensure that your audio is neither too loud nor too soft. Normalize your audio tracks to achieve a consistent volume throughout your video. Proper audio balancing enhances the viewer experience.

Adding background music and sound effects enhances your videos. Music sets the tone and mood, while sound effects add realism and interest. Choose royalty-free music and sound effects that complement your content. Balance the volume of your background audio with your main audio to avoid distractions.

Using audio transitions and fades creates a smooth listening experience. Audio transitions like crossfades and fade-ins/outs help blend different audio clips seamlessly. Use these transitions to avoid abrupt changes in audio that can distract viewers. Smooth audio transitions enhance the overall quality of your videos.

Tips for recording voiceovers include using a quiet space, speaking clearly, and using proper microphone technique. Voiceovers should be recorded in a controlled environment with minimal background noise. Use a pop filter and speak at a consistent volume and pace. Editing your voiceover ensures that it's clear and professional.

The impact of audio on viewer engagement cannot be overstated. High-quality audio keeps viewers engaged and enhances their overall experience. Clear and professional sound helps convey your message effectively and keeps viewers interested. Invest in good audio equipment and techniques to improve viewer retention.

Reviewing and improving your audio setup is an ongoing process. Regularly test and adjust your equipment and settings to achieve the best results. Experiment with different microphones, placements, and editing techniques to find what works best for your content. Continuous improvement ensures that your audio remains high-quality and professional.

The importance of audio testing cannot be overstated. Test your audio setup before each filming session to ensure everything is working correctly. Record a short test clip and review the audio for any issues. Regular testing helps you identify and resolve problems before they affect your final recording.

Recording interviews and multiple audio sources requires proper setup and coordination. Use multiple microphones to capture clear audio from all participants. Mix and balance the audio tracks in post-production to ensure that each voice is clear and distinct. Proper setup and editing ensure high-quality interview recordings.

Using lavalier and shotgun microphones offers flexibility and versatility. Lavalier microphones are great for hands-free recording and capturing clear audio from a distance. Shotgun microphones provide directional audio capture, making them ideal for focused sound recording. Choose the right microphone for your filming needs.

The role of audio interfaces and mixers in professional audio recording is significant. Audio interfaces connect your microphones to your computer, providing high-quality audio capture. Mixers allow you to adjust audio levels and add effects in real-time. These tools enhance your audio setup and provide more control over your recordings.

Capturing high-quality audio on a budget is possible with the right tools and techniques. Invest in affordable yet reliable microphones, use free audio editing software, and create a simple soundproofing setup. Prioritize audio quality within your budget to achieve professional results.

Maintaining and caring for your audio equipment prolongs its lifespan and ensures optimal performance. Regularly clean your microphones, cables, and accessories to prevent dust and dirt buildup. Store your equipment in a safe, dry place and handle it with care. Proper maintenance keeps your gear in top condition and ready for recording.

Final tips for setting up your audio include investing in good equipment, understanding audio techniques, and practicing regularly. Enjoy the process of creating high-quality sound for your videos. With the right setup and techniques, you can produce professional audio that enhances your content and engages your audience.

Chapter 14: Set Up Your Lighting

The importance of good lighting in video production cannot be overstated. Proper lighting enhances the quality of your videos, making them more visually appealing and professional. Good lighting ensures that your subject is well-lit, colors are accurate, and details are clear. Investing in quality lighting equipment and techniques is essential for creating high-quality content.

Understanding different types of lighting helps you choose the best setup for your needs. Key lighting, fill lighting, and backlighting are the three main types of lighting used in video production. Key lighting is the primary source of light, fill lighting reduces shadows, and backlighting separates the subject from the background. Using these three types of lighting creates a balanced and professional look.

Choosing the right lighting setup involves selecting the appropriate lights and accessories. Softbox lights, ring lights, and LED panels are popular choices for YouTubers. Softbox lights provide soft, even lighting, while ring lights create flattering, shadow-free light. LED panels offer versatility and portability. Choose lights that suit your filming style and environment.

Setting up softbox lights and ring lights ensures that your subject is well-lit. Position your key light at a 45-degree angle to your subject to create a natural look. Use fill lights to reduce shadows and backlights to add depth. Experiment with different placements to achieve the desired effect. Proper setup enhances the overall quality of your videos.

Using natural light for filming is a cost-effective and convenient option. Natural light provides a soft and flattering look, especially during the golden hour (shortly after sunrise or before sunset). Position your subject near a window to take advantage of natural light. Use reflectors to bounce light and reduce shadows. Natural light is an excellent option for beginners and on-the-go filming.

The role of color temperature in lighting is significant. Color temperature affects the mood and tone of your videos. Warm light (yellow) creates a cozy and inviting atmosphere, while cool light (blue) provides a modern and clean look. Use adjustable lights or gels to control color temperature. Matching the color temperature of your lights ensures consistency and professionalism.

Techniques for three-point lighting create a balanced and professional look. Three-point lighting involves using key, fill, and backlighting to illuminate your subject from different angles. This setup reduces shadows, highlights details, and adds depth. Experiment with different positions and intensities to achieve the desired effect.

Avoiding common lighting mistakes is essential for high-quality production. Overexposure, underexposure, and harsh shadows can detract from your videos. Use diffusers and reflectors to soften light and reduce shadows. Adjust your camera settings to avoid overexposure. Addressing these common issues improves your video quality.

Using reflectors and diffusers helps control and manipulate light. Reflectors bounce light to fill in shadows and add highlights, while diffusers soften harsh light and create even illumination. These inexpensive accessories are valuable tools for achieving professional lighting. Experiment with different reflectors and diffusers to enhance your setup.

Adjusting lighting for different environments requires adaptability. Indoor and outdoor environments present unique lighting challenges. Use artificial lights to supplement natural light indoors, and adjust your setup based on the available light. Outdoor filming requires consideration of changing light conditions and weather. Being adaptable ensures that your lighting is always optimal.

Balancing lighting for consistent quality is crucial. Ensure that your key, fill, and backlighting are balanced to create an even and flattering look. Use light meters or your camera's exposure settings to measure and adjust the intensity of your lights. Consistent lighting enhances the overall quality of your videos.

Creating mood and atmosphere with lighting adds interest and engagement. Use color gels, lighting angles, and intensity to create different moods. Warm light creates a cozy and inviting atmosphere, while cool light provides a modern and clean look. Experiment with different lighting setups to match the tone of your content.

The impact of lighting on video quality cannot be overstated. Proper lighting enhances the visual appeal, clarity, and professionalism of your videos. Good lighting highlights details, improves color accuracy, and reduces shadows. Investing in quality lighting equipment and techniques is essential for creating high-quality content.

Setting up lighting for green screen filming requires proper setup and positioning. Use evenly distributed lights to eliminate shadows and ensure that the green screen is uniformly lit. Position your subject at a distance from the green screen to avoid casting shadows. Proper lighting ensures that your green screen footage is clean and easy to edit.

Using LED panels and portable lights provides versatility and convenience. LED panels offer adjustable brightness and color temperature, making them ideal for various filming scenarios. Portable lights are great for on-the-go filming and can be easily transported. Investing in LED panels and portable lights enhances your lighting setup.

Managing shadows and highlights ensures that your subject is well-lit and details are clear. Use fill lights and reflectors to reduce harsh shadows, and adjust your key light to highlight important features. Proper shadow management creates a balanced and professional look.

Tips for low-light filming include using high-ISO settings, wide apertures, and additional lighting. Low-light conditions can be challenging, but proper techniques and equipment can improve your results. Use noise reduction tools in post-production to enhance low-light footage. Understanding how to work with low light ensures that your videos are clear and professional.

Maintaining and caring for your lighting equipment prolongs its lifespan and ensures optimal performance. Regularly clean your lights, cables, and accessories to prevent dust and dirt buildup. Store your equipment in a safe, dry place and handle it with care. Proper maintenance keeps your gear in top condition and ready for filming.

Troubleshooting common lighting issues helps you address problems quickly and efficiently. Issues like flickering lights, color balance problems, and shadows can be frustrating. Learn basic troubleshooting techniques to resolve these issues on the spot. Being prepared ensures that you can handle any challenges during filming.

The importance of lighting tests cannot be overstated. Test your lighting setup before each filming session to ensure everything is working correctly. Record a short test clip and review the lighting for any issues. Regular testing helps you identify and resolve problems before they affect your final recording.

Upgrading your lighting setup over time ensures that your videos remain high-quality and professional. As your skills and needs evolve, invest in better lights, accessories, and techniques. Regularly review and update your lighting setup to match your growing expertise and content quality.

Creative lighting techniques add interest and engagement to your videos. Experiment with different lighting angles, colors, and effects to create unique and visually appealing content. Creative lighting enhances your storytelling and keeps viewers engaged.

Using smart lighting systems provides convenience and flexibility. Smart lights offer remote control, adjustable color temperature, and programmable settings. These features allow you to easily customize your lighting setup and create consistent results. Investing in smart lighting systems enhances your production quality.

The role of lighting in visual storytelling is significant. Proper lighting sets the tone, highlights important details, and enhances the overall mood of your videos. Use lighting to convey emotions, create atmosphere, and support your narrative. Understanding the impact of lighting on storytelling improves your content.

Final tips for setting up your lighting include investing in quality equipment, understanding lighting techniques, and practicing regularly. Enjoy the process of creating high-quality visuals for your videos. With the right setup and techniques, you can produce professional lighting that enhances your content and engages your audience.

Chapter 15: Perfect Your Background

The importance of a clean and professional background in video production cannot be overstated. A well-thought-out background enhances the visual appeal of your videos, adds context, and helps maintain viewer attention. A cluttered or distracting background can detract from your content and make your videos appear unprofessional.

Choosing the right background for your videos involves selecting a setting that complements your subject and aligns with your brand. Consider using simple, neutral backgrounds that keep the focus on you. Alternatively, choose a background that reflects your content theme or personal style. The right background enhances the overall look and feel of your videos.

Setting up a backdrop or green screen provides versatility and control over your background. Backdrops come in various colors and designs, allowing you to create a consistent look for your videos. Green screens enable you to replace the background with any image or video during post-production. Both options offer professional-looking backgrounds and enhance your production quality.

Using your environment as a background adds a personal touch to your videos. Filming in your home, office, or other familiar settings creates a relatable and authentic look. Ensure that your environment is clean, organized, and free from distractions. Personal environments provide context and make your videos more engaging.

Techniques for decluttering your background help maintain a clean and professional appearance. Remove any unnecessary items, organize your space, and keep the focus on your subject. A clutter-free background reduces distractions and enhances the viewer experience. Regularly review and tidy your filming area to maintain a professional look.

Adding personal touches to your background makes your videos more relatable. Use props, decorations, and personal items that reflect your personality and brand. These elements add interest and create a unique look for your videos. Personal touches make your content more engaging and memorable.

Balancing background elements with your subject ensures that your videos are visually appealing. Avoid backgrounds that are too busy or overpowering. Use colors, patterns, and decorations that complement your subject without distracting from it. A balanced background enhances the overall quality of your videos.

Using props and decorations effectively adds context and interest to your videos. Props can illustrate points, add visual variety, and create a cohesive look. Use decorations to enhance the overall aesthetic and support your content theme. Thoughtfully chosen props and decorations enhance viewer engagement.

The role of background lighting is significant in creating a professional look. Use backlighting to separate your subject from the background and add depth. Ensure that your background is evenly lit to avoid harsh shadows and distractions. Proper background lighting enhances the overall visual quality of your videos.

Creating depth and dimension with your background adds visual interest. Use elements like furniture, plants, and decorations to create layers and depth. Position these elements strategically to add dimension without cluttering the frame. Depth and dimension make your videos more visually appealing and professional.

Tips for shooting in small spaces include using strategic angles, lighting, and props. Small spaces can be challenging, but with careful planning, you can create a professional look. Use wide-angle lenses to capture more of the space, and position your lights to maximize the available area. Small space filming requires creativity and adaptability.

The impact of background on viewer perception is significant. A clean, organized background conveys professionalism and attention to detail. Conversely, a cluttered or messy background can create a negative impression.

Ensuring that your background reflects your brand and content theme enhances viewer perception.

Setting up a dedicated filming space provides consistency and convenience. Having a designated area for filming ensures that your background is always ready and reduces setup time. Customize your filming space to reflect your brand and content style. A dedicated space enhances your overall production quality.

Using virtual backgrounds and effects adds versatility to your videos. Virtual backgrounds allow you to change your setting without physical changes. Use software or green screens to create virtual backgrounds that enhance your content. Virtual backgrounds provide flexibility and creativity.

Adjusting your background for different types of videos ensures consistency and relevance. Different video formats, such as tutorials, vlogs, and interviews, may require different backgrounds. Customize your background to suit the specific content and maintain a professional look. Adapting your background enhances the viewer experience.

The importance of consistency in your background cannot be overstated. Consistent backgrounds create a cohesive look and reinforce your brand identity. Regularly review and update your background to ensure it aligns with your content and style. Consistency enhances viewer recognition and trust.

Experimenting with different background styles can help you find what works best for your content. Try various setups, props, and decorations to see what resonates with your audience. Regularly update and refresh your background to keep it interesting and relevant. Experimentation fosters creativity and improvement.

Incorporating branding elements into your background strengthens your brand identity. Use logos, colors, and other brand elements to create a cohesive look. These elements reinforce your brand and make your videos more recognizable. Branding in your background enhances viewer engagement and loyalty.

Reviewing and improving your background setup is an ongoing process. Regularly assess your background for clutter, distractions, and alignment with your brand. Make necessary adjustments to enhance the overall quality of your videos. Continuous improvement ensures that your background remains professional and engaging.

Tips for shooting on location include planning your setup, managing lighting, and minimizing distractions. On-location filming can add variety and context to your videos. Choose locations that align with your content and brand, and ensure that your setup is professional. On-location filming requires adaptability and preparation.

Using background to enhance storytelling adds depth and interest to your videos. Background elements can provide context, illustrate points, and create a mood. Use your background to support your narrative and engage viewers. Thoughtful background design enhances your storytelling and overall content quality.

The role of background in visual aesthetics is significant. A well-designed background enhances the visual appeal of your videos and creates a professional look. Use colors, patterns, and decorations that complement your subject and content. Visual aesthetics contribute to viewer engagement and retention.

Maintaining a versatile background setup provides flexibility for different types of content. Use modular elements that can be easily rearranged and customized. Versatility ensures that your background remains relevant and engaging for various video formats. A flexible setup enhances your overall production quality.

The impact of background on video quality cannot be overstated. A clean, organized, and well-lit background enhances the overall quality of your videos. Investing time and effort into creating a professional background improves viewer perception and engagement. A high-quality background is essential for successful video production.

Final tips for perfecting your background include investing in quality elements, understanding background techniques, and practicing regularly. Enjoy the process of creating and refining your background setup. With the right setup and techniques, you can produce professional and engaging videos that captivate your audience.

Chapter 16: Exclusive Bonus Materials

———

Offering exclusive content to your audience is a powerful way to build loyalty and engagement. Exclusive bonus materials provide added value and create a sense of appreciation among your viewers. These materials can include bonus videos, behind-the-scenes footage, downloadable resources, and more. By offering exclusive content, you can deepen your connection with your audience and encourage them to support your channel further.

Creating bonus videos and behind-the-scenes footage gives your audience a peek into your creative process. Bonus videos can include bloopers, extended content, or special topics that aren't part of your regular uploads. Behind-the-scenes footage showcases how you create your videos, offering insights and a personal touch. These exclusive videos make your audience feel special and more connected to you.

Developing downloadable resources and guides adds value to your content. These materials can include eBooks, worksheets, templates, and checklists that complement your videos. Offering exclusive downloads provides additional learning tools and enhances your audience's experience. Downloadable resources are a valuable addition to your content strategy.

Using platforms like Patreon and membership sites allows you to offer exclusive content to your most dedicated fans. These platforms enable you to create tiered memberships with different levels of access and benefits. By offering exclusive content through Patreon or similar services, you can monetize your channel and reward your loyal supporters.

Offering early access to new content is another way to provide exclusivity. Allow your most dedicated viewers to watch your videos before they're publicly released. Early access creates a sense of privilege and appreciation among your audience. It also encourages more viewers to become dedicated fans to gain access to this perk.

Creating merchandise and branded products is a great way to engage with your audience and generate revenue. Design and sell products like T-shirts, mugs, stickers, and more that reflect your brand and content. Merchandise allows your fans to show their support and feel connected to your channel. Branded products also serve as promotional tools.

Engaging with your audience through live streams offers real-time interaction and exclusivity. Use live streams to answer questions, share updates, and connect with your viewers on a personal level. Live streaming provides a unique opportunity to engage with your audience directly and build a stronger community.

The importance of adding value for your audience cannot be overstated. Exclusive content should provide genuine value and enhance the viewer experience. Whether it's additional learning materials, personal interactions, or special insights, ensure that your exclusive content is meaningful and valuable to your audience.

Creating special series and collaborations adds variety and interest to your channel. Develop a series of videos around a specific theme or topic, and collaborate with other creators to bring fresh perspectives. Special series and collaborations provide exclusive content that keeps your audience engaged and excited.

Offering personalized content and shout-outs makes your audience feel appreciated. Personalized videos, messages, and shout-outs acknowledge your most dedicated fans and strengthen their connection to your channel. This personal touch fosters loyalty and encourages continued support.

The role of exclusive content in building loyalty is significant. By offering special access and benefits, you create a sense of community and appreciation among your viewers. Exclusive content encourages viewers to support your channel and stay engaged with your content.

Using email newsletters for exclusive updates keeps your audience informed and engaged. Send regular newsletters with exclusive content, behind-the-scenes insights, and updates on your channel. Newsletters provide a direct line of communication with your audience and enhance their connection to your content.

Creating private groups and communities offers a space for dedicated fans to connect and engage. Platforms like Facebook Groups or Discord servers allow you to create exclusive communities where viewers can interact with you and each other. Private groups foster a sense of belonging and loyalty among your audience.

Offering courses and workshops provides valuable learning opportunities. Develop online courses or workshops that dive deeper into your content topics. These educational offerings provide exclusive value and position you as an authority in your niche. Courses and workshops are a great way to monetize your expertise and engage your audience.

Providing exclusive discounts and offers rewards your loyal viewers. Offer special discounts on merchandise, courses, or other products and services. Exclusive offers create a sense of appreciation and encourage viewers to support your channel further.

The impact of exclusive content on channel growth is significant. Exclusive materials attract dedicated fans, increase engagement, and encourage monetization. By offering added value, you can build a loyal community that supports your channel's growth and success.

Collecting feedback on bonus materials helps you improve and refine your exclusive content. Ask your audience for their opinions on the value and relevance of your bonus materials. Use this feedback to make adjustments and enhance the overall experience. Regularly updating and improving your exclusive content ensures that it remains valuable and engaging.

Promoting your exclusive content is essential for attracting dedicated fans. Use your regular videos, social media, and email newsletters to highlight the benefits of your exclusive materials. Encourage viewers to support your channel and gain access to these special perks. Effective promotion increases awareness and engagement.

Balancing free and exclusive content is crucial for maintaining a broad audience while rewarding your most dedicated fans. Ensure that your regular content remains valuable and accessible to all viewers, while offering exclusive materials as added value. This balance ensures that you retain a wide audience while fostering loyalty among your core supporters.

The role of exclusivity in audience engagement cannot be overstated. Exclusive content creates a sense of privilege and appreciation among your viewers. By offering special access and benefits, you can deepen your connection with your audience and encourage continued support.

Using analytics to refine your bonus materials provides valuable insights into what resonates with your audience. Track the performance of your exclusive content and use this data to make informed decisions. Analytics help you understand what your viewers value and how to enhance their experience.

Collaborating with other creators for exclusive content offers fresh perspectives and new opportunities. Partner with other YouTubers to create special series, workshops, or events. Collaborations introduce your channel to new audiences and provide unique value to your viewers.

Offering exclusive content on multiple platforms broadens your reach and engagement. Use Patreon, membership sites, social media, and your website to provide exclusive materials. This multi-platform approach ensures that your exclusive content reaches a wider audience and enhances your overall engagement.

The importance of consistency in exclusive content cannot be overstated. Regularly update and refresh your exclusive materials to keep them valuable and relevant. Consistent exclusive content maintains viewer interest and encourages continued support.

Final tips for creating exclusive bonus materials include providing genuine value, promoting your content effectively, and regularly updating your materials. Enjoy the process of creating special content for your dedicated fans. With the right approach, exclusive bonus materials enhance your channel's engagement and growth.

Chapter 17: Talk to the Camera

―――

Building confidence in front of the camera is essential for creating engaging YouTube videos. Many creators feel nervous or awkward when they first start filming, but practice and preparation can help overcome these feelings. Techniques for engaging with your audience include maintaining eye contact, using natural body language, and speaking clearly.

The importance of eye contact and body language cannot be overstated. Eye contact helps build a connection with your viewers and makes your delivery more engaging. Natural body language, such as gestures and facial expressions, enhances your communication and makes your content more dynamic. Practice maintaining eye contact with the camera and using expressive body language.

Practicing your delivery and tone helps improve your on-camera presence. Record yourself speaking on different topics and review the footage to identify areas for improvement. Focus on your tone, pacing, and clarity. The more you practice, the more comfortable and confident you'll become.

Using prompts and notes effectively can help you stay on track without sounding scripted. Bullet points or key phrases can guide your speaking while allowing for a natural delivery. Place your notes near the camera to maintain eye contact with your viewers. Prompts help you cover all key points while keeping your delivery conversational.

The role of spontaneity and authenticity in your delivery is significant. While preparation is important, allowing for spontaneous moments makes your content more relatable and genuine. Don't be afraid to show your personality and react naturally during filming. Authenticity builds trust and engagement with your audience.

Overcoming nervousness and camera shyness requires practice and positive reinforcement. Start by filming short clips and gradually increase the length and complexity of your videos. Focus on your passion for the content and the value you're providing to your viewers. Positive feedback and incremental progress boost your confidence.

Developing a connection with your viewers involves speaking directly to them and addressing their interests and concerns. Use a friendly and approachable tone, and imagine you're having a conversation with a friend. A personal and relatable approach fosters a strong connection with your audience.

Techniques for natural and conversational delivery include using simple language, avoiding jargon, and varying your tone. Speak as you would in a casual conversation, and use examples and anecdotes to illustrate your points. A conversational delivery makes your content more engaging and easier to understand.

Practicing with mock interviews and role-playing can help you improve your on-camera presence. Enlist a friend or family member to act as an interviewer or audience member. Practice answering questions and discussing topics in a natural and confident manner. Role-playing builds confidence and improves your communication skills.

Using humor and personality in your delivery makes your videos more enjoyable. Incorporate light-hearted moments and humor to keep your content entertaining. Let your personality shine through to create a unique and memorable viewing experience. Humor and personality enhance viewer engagement and retention.

Managing your energy and enthusiasm is crucial for maintaining viewer interest. While it's important to be energetic, avoid overacting or coming across as insincere. Find a balance that reflects your genuine enthusiasm for the content. Consistent energy keeps your audience engaged and interested.

The impact of storytelling on viewer engagement cannot be overstated. Use personal stories, anecdotes, and examples to illustrate your points and make your content more relatable. Storytelling creates an emotional connection with your viewers and enhances their engagement with your videos.

Practicing active listening and responsiveness during live streams and Q&A sessions builds a strong connection with your audience. Pay attention to viewer comments and questions, and respond thoughtfully. Active listening shows that you value your audience's input and enhances their engagement.

The importance of a clear and concise message cannot be overstated. Stay focused on your main points and avoid unnecessary tangents. A clear and concise delivery ensures that your viewers understand and retain the information you're presenting. Clarity and focus enhance the overall quality of your videos.

Using vocal variety and pacing keeps your delivery dynamic and interesting. Vary your tone, pitch, and speed to emphasize key points and maintain viewer interest. Avoid speaking in a monotone or rushing through your content. Vocal variety adds interest and engagement to your videos.

Practicing facial expressions and gestures enhances your on-camera presence. Use expressive facial expressions to convey emotions and emphasize your points. Gestures add movement and interest to your delivery. Practice using natural and appropriate expressions and gestures to enhance your communication.

Handling interruptions and distractions during filming requires patience and adaptability. If interruptions occur, pause and address them calmly before continuing. Edit out any distractions during post-production. Maintaining composure and focus ensures a smooth and professional delivery.

Recording practice sessions for self-review helps you identify areas for improvement. Watch your recordings and critique your delivery, body language, and overall presence. Use this feedback to make adjustments and refine your on-camera skills. Regular practice and review enhance your performance.

Seeking feedback from trusted peers provides valuable insights and encouragement. Share your videos with friends, family, or fellow creators and ask for constructive feedback. Use their input to identify strengths and areas for improvement. Peer feedback supports your growth and confidence.

Adapting your style based on audience feedback ensures that your content remains relevant and engaging. Pay attention to viewer comments and suggestions, and adjust your delivery accordingly. Regularly reviewing and incorporating feedback helps you connect with your audience and improve your content.

Techniques for maintaining audience attention include using visual aids, varying your delivery, and engaging with viewers. Visual aids like slides, graphics, and props add interest and support your content. Engage with your audience by asking questions and encouraging interaction. These techniques enhance viewer retention and engagement.

The importance of a strong opening and closing cannot be overstated. Start with a compelling introduction that hooks your viewers and clearly states what the video is about. End with a strong closing that summarizes key points and encourages viewers to take action. A strong opening and closing enhance the overall impact of your videos.

Practicing empathy and relatability in your delivery builds a strong connection with your audience. Show empathy by addressing viewer concerns and experiences. Relatability comes from sharing personal stories and speaking in a conversational tone. Empathy and relatability foster trust and engagement with your audience.

The role of spontaneity and authenticity in your delivery is significant. While preparation is important, allowing for spontaneous moments makes your content more relatable and genuine. Don't be afraid to show your personality and react naturally during filming. Authenticity builds trust and engagement with your audience.

Final tips for effective on-camera communication include practicing regularly, seeking feedback, and embracing your unique style. Enjoy the process of creating and sharing your content. With the right techniques and practice, you can develop a confident and engaging on-camera presence that captivates your audience.

Chapter 18: Set Up Your First Video

Setting up your first video is an exciting step in your YouTube journey. Proper planning and preparation ensure that your video is engaging, professional, and aligned with your goals. Begin by planning your video concept. Think about what topic you want to cover, who your target audience is, and what message you want to convey. A clear concept sets the foundation for a successful video.

Writing a script or outline helps organize your thoughts and ensures that you cover all key points. Depending on your style, you can write a detailed script or use bullet points to guide your speaking. A script provides structure and helps you stay on track during filming. It also reduces the likelihood of forgetting important information.

Setting up your filming location is the next step. Choose a quiet, well-lit space where you feel comfortable and free from distractions. Ensure that your background is clean, organized, and aligned with your content theme. A professional and visually appealing setup enhances the overall quality of your video.

Preparing your equipment and tools is essential for smooth filming. Gather your camera, microphone, lighting, and any other necessary accessories. Ensure that your equipment is in good working condition and that you have all the necessary cables and batteries. Proper preparation prevents technical issues and ensures a smooth filming process.

Testing your camera and audio setup helps identify any potential issues before you start filming. Record a short test clip and review the footage for clarity, lighting, and audio quality. Adjust your settings and setup as needed to achieve the best results. Testing ensures that your final video is high-quality and professional.

Arranging your lighting is crucial for creating a well-lit and visually appealing video. Use key, fill, and backlighting to illuminate your subject from different angles. Experiment with different lighting setups to achieve the desired effect. Proper lighting enhances the overall quality and professionalism of your video.

Setting up your background is another important step. Choose a clean and organized background that complements your subject. Use props and decorations to add interest and context to your video. A well-thought-out background enhances the overall aesthetic and keeps viewers engaged.

Practicing your delivery helps improve your on-camera presence. Rehearse your script or outline multiple times to become familiar with your content. Focus on your tone, pacing, and body language. The more you practice, the more confident and natural you'll appear on camera.

Recording test shots helps ensure that your setup is optimal. Record a few test clips to check for framing, lighting, and audio quality. Review the footage and make any necessary adjustments. Test shots help you identify and resolve issues before you start filming your final video.

Finalizing your video plan involves reviewing your concept, script, and setup. Ensure that everything is aligned with your goals and that you're prepared for a smooth filming process. A clear and well-thought-out plan sets the stage for a successful video.

Preparing for potential challenges helps you stay adaptable and ready to handle any issues that arise. Think about potential obstacles, such as technical difficulties or interruptions, and have a plan in place to address them. Being prepared ensures that you can handle challenges efficiently and continue filming smoothly.

Ensuring a smooth filming process involves staying organized and focused. Follow your script or outline, stay on track, and avoid unnecessary distractions. Take breaks if needed, but stay focused on your goal. A smooth filming process enhances the overall quality of your video.

Techniques for staying calm and focused during filming include deep breathing, visualization, and positive self-talk. Take a few deep breaths before you start filming to calm your nerves. Visualize yourself speaking confidently and engaging with your audience. Use positive affirmations to boost your confidence.

Recording the introduction and hook is the first step in filming your video. Start with a compelling introduction that grabs your viewers' attention and clearly states what the video is about. The hook should engage your audience and encourage them to keep watching. A strong introduction sets the tone for the rest of your video.

Filming the main content involves covering all the key points in your script or outline. Stay focused on your message, and use clear and concise language. Incorporate visual aids, examples, and storytelling to enhance your content. Engaging and informative content keeps viewers interested and engaged.

Recording transitions and additional shots helps create a smooth and cohesive video. Use transitions to connect different segments of your video and maintain viewer engagement. Additional shots, such as B-roll or cutaways, add variety and context to your content. Thoughtful transitions and additional shots enhance the overall quality of your video.

Wrapping up your video involves summarizing the key points and encouraging viewers to take action. Use a clear and concise closing statement that reinforces your message. Include a call to action, such as liking, commenting, subscribing, or visiting a website. A strong closing leaves a lasting impression and encourages further engagement.

Reviewing the footage helps identify any issues and areas for improvement. Watch your recorded clips and look for clarity, lighting, and audio quality. Make any necessary adjustments and re-record segments if needed. Reviewing ensures that your final video is high-quality and professional.

Making necessary adjustments involves refining your setup, delivery, and content. Use the feedback from your review to make improvements. Adjust your lighting, audio, or framing as needed. Making adjustments ensures that your final video meets your standards and goals.

Preparing for the editing process involves organizing your footage and gathering any additional materials. Transfer your clips to your computer and create a folder for easy access. Gather any graphics, music, or other elements you plan to use. Proper preparation streamlines the editing process.

Techniques for a successful first video shoot include staying organized, practicing regularly, and being adaptable. Follow your plan, stay focused, and make necessary adjustments. Enjoy the process of creating and sharing your content. With the right approach, your first video shoot will be a positive and successful experience.

Common pitfalls to avoid include overcomplicating your setup, neglecting preparation, and getting discouraged by mistakes. Keep your setup simple and focus on the essentials. Prepare thoroughly and stay positive, even if things don't go perfectly. Avoiding these pitfalls ensures a smooth and enjoyable filming process.

Final thoughts on creating your first video include celebrating your progress, learning from your experiences, and staying motivated. Enjoy the process of creating and sharing your content. With dedication and effort, your YouTube channel will grow and thrive. Your first video is just the beginning of an exciting and rewarding journey.

Chapter 19: Shoot Your First Video

———

Setting up your filming space is the first step in shooting your first video. Choose a quiet, well-lit area where you feel comfortable and free from distractions. Ensure that your background is clean, organized, and aligned with your content theme. A professional and visually appealing setup enhances the overall quality of your video.

Adjusting your camera settings is crucial for achieving high-quality footage. Use the highest resolution and frame rate available on your camera or phone. Adjust settings like exposure, focus, and white balance to match the lighting conditions. Proper camera settings ensure that your footage is clear, well-lit, and visually appealing.

Preparing your script and talking points helps organize your thoughts and ensures that you cover all key points. Depending on your style, you can write a detailed script or use bullet points to guide your speaking. A script provides structure and helps you stay on track during filming. It also reduces the likelihood of forgetting important information.

Recording a strong introduction sets the tone for your video. Start with a compelling introduction that grabs your viewers' attention and clearly states what the video is about. The hook should engage your audience and encourage them to keep watching. A strong introduction sets the stage for a successful video.

Techniques for smooth transitions help create a cohesive and engaging video. Use transitions to connect different segments of your video and maintain viewer engagement. Additional shots, such as B-roll or cutaways, add variety and context to your content. Thoughtful transitions and additional shots enhance the overall quality of your video.

Capturing different angles and shots adds visual interest and variety to your video. Experiment with various perspectives, such as close-ups, wide shots, and over-the-shoulder angles. Different angles create a dynamic and engaging viewing experience. Use a tripod or stabilizer to keep your shots steady and professional.

Using B-roll footage enhances your main content and provides additional context. B-roll is supplementary footage that adds variety and visual interest to your video. Use B-roll to illustrate points, cover cuts, and add depth to your content. High-quality B-roll improves the overall production value of your video.

Recording clear audio is essential for engaging and professional videos. Use an external microphone to capture high-quality audio and reduce background noise. Position the microphone close to your mouth but out of the frame. Clear and professional audio enhances the viewer experience and keeps them engaged.

Keeping your energy consistent throughout filming helps maintain viewer interest. While it's important to be energetic, avoid overacting or coming across as insincere. Find a balance that reflects your genuine enthusiasm for the content. Consistent energy keeps your audience engaged and interested.

Managing time effectively during filming ensures that you stay on track and avoid unnecessary delays. Plan your filming schedule and allocate enough time for each segment. Take breaks if needed, but stay focused on your goals. Effective time management enhances the overall quality of your video.

Recording multiple takes if needed allows for flexibility and refinement. Don't be afraid to re-record segments if you're not satisfied with the first take. Multiple takes provide more options during editing and ensure that your final video is polished and professional.

Reviewing and adjusting during the shoot helps identify and resolve issues on the spot. Watch your recorded clips and look for clarity, lighting, and audio quality. Make any necessary adjustments and re-record segments if needed. Reviewing ensures that your final video meets your standards and goals.

Staying flexible and adaptable during filming is crucial for handling unexpected challenges. Be prepared to adjust your setup, delivery, and content as needed. Adaptability ensures that you can handle any obstacles and continue filming smoothly.

Techniques for engaging delivery include using clear language, natural body language, and expressive facial expressions. Speak clearly and at a consistent pace, and use gestures to emphasize key points. An engaging delivery keeps your viewers interested and enhances the overall quality of your video.

Managing lighting changes during filming ensures consistent quality. Adjust your lighting setup based on the available light and any changes in the environment. Use additional lights or reflectors to maintain even illumination. Proper lighting management enhances the overall visual appeal of your video.

Ensuring continuity in your footage involves maintaining a consistent look and feel throughout your video. Pay attention to details like clothing, background, and lighting to avoid continuity errors. Consistent footage creates a cohesive and professional viewing experience.

Using visual aids and props adds interest and context to your video. Visual aids, such as slides, graphics, and physical props, support your content and enhance viewer understanding. Thoughtfully chosen visual aids improve engagement and add variety to your videos.

Capturing high-quality video and audio ensures that your content is professional and engaging. Use the right equipment, techniques, and settings to achieve the best results. High-quality production enhances viewer satisfaction and retention.

Techniques for maintaining focus include staying organized, following your script, and avoiding distractions. Stay focused on your message and avoid unnecessary tangents. Clear and concise delivery ensures that your viewers understand and retain the information you're presenting.

Handling on-camera mistakes with confidence and composure is essential for a smooth filming process. If you make a mistake, pause, correct it, and continue filming. Editing can remove minor errors, so focus on maintaining a positive and confident delivery. Handling mistakes gracefully enhances your on-camera presence.

Keeping your setup organized ensures a smooth and efficient filming process. Arrange your equipment, props, and notes in an orderly manner to minimize distractions and disruptions. An organized setup enhances your productivity and overall quality of your video.

Reviewing the footage for quality involves watching your recorded clips and identifying any issues. Look for clarity, lighting, and audio quality, and make any necessary adjustments. Regular review ensures that your final video is polished and professional.

Making necessary reshoots involves re-recording segments that don't meet your standards. Use the feedback from your review to make improvements and ensure that your content is high-quality. Reshoots provide more options during editing and enhance the overall quality of your video.

Preparing for the editing process involves organizing your footage and gathering any additional materials. Transfer your clips to your computer and create a folder for easy access. Gather any graphics, music, or other elements you plan to use. Proper preparation streamlines the editing process.

Final tips for shooting your first video include staying organized, practicing regularly, and being adaptable. Enjoy the process of creating and sharing your content. With the right techniques and practice, you can produce high-quality videos that captivate your audience.

Chapter 20: Shoot Your B-Roll

Understanding the importance of B-roll footage is essential for creating engaging and dynamic videos. B-roll is supplementary footage that enhances your main content by adding visual interest, context, and variety. It helps illustrate points, cover cuts, and create a more professional and polished video. Incorporating B-roll into your videos improves overall production quality and keeps viewers engaged.

Planning your B-roll shots involves identifying key moments and elements that will enhance your main content. Think about what supplementary footage will add value to your video and help convey your message. Create a shot list or storyboard to guide your filming and ensure you capture all necessary B-roll footage. Proper planning ensures that your B-roll is purposeful and effective.

Techniques for capturing high-quality B-roll include using stable shots, varied angles, and smooth camera movements. Use a tripod or stabilizer to keep your shots steady and professional. Experiment with different perspectives, such as close-ups, wide shots, and dynamic angles. Smooth camera movements, such as pans and tilts, add interest and visual appeal to your B-roll.

Using B-roll to enhance your story involves selecting footage that supports and complements your main content. B-roll can illustrate points, provide context, and add depth to your narrative. Choose clips that are relevant and enhance the overall message of your video. Thoughtfully chosen B-roll enhances viewer engagement and understanding.

Recording different types of B-roll provides variety and interest. Consider capturing establishing shots, action shots, cutaways, and detailed close-ups. Establishing shots set the scene and provide context, while action shots show dynamic movements and interactions. Cutaways add variety and break up the main content, while close-ups highlight details and add visual interest.

Tips for filming dynamic B-roll shots include using movement, experimenting with angles, and incorporating different perspectives. Use techniques like tracking shots, zooms, and slow motion to add variety and interest to your B-roll. Experiment with different angles, such as low angles, high angles, and over-the-shoulder shots. Dynamic B-roll keeps your videos visually engaging and professional.

Integrating B-roll with your main footage involves seamlessly blending the two to create a cohesive and engaging video. Use transitions, overlays, and cuts to incorporate B-roll naturally into your main content. Ensure that your B-roll supports and enhances your narrative without distracting from it. Smooth integration of B-roll improves the overall quality of your video.

Using B-roll for transitions and effects adds visual interest and variety to your videos. B-roll can serve as a bridge between different segments of your video, creating smooth transitions and maintaining viewer engagement. Incorporate effects like slow motion, time-lapse, and overlays to enhance your B-roll and add a professional touch.

Techniques for smooth B-roll integration include using transitions, matching colors and lighting, and maintaining continuity. Use transitions like crossfades, dissolves, and cuts to blend B-roll seamlessly with your main footage. Ensure that the colors and lighting in your B-roll match your main footage to create a consistent look. Maintaining continuity ensures that your B-roll supports your narrative without causing distractions.

Reviewing and organizing your B-roll footage helps streamline the editing process. Transfer your B-roll clips to your computer and create a folder for easy access. Review each clip for quality, relevance, and potential use in your video. Organize your footage into categories based on themes, scenes, or segments. Proper organization saves time and ensures that you can easily find and use your B-roll during editing.

Adjusting your B-roll setup involves refining your equipment, techniques, and shot list based on your review. Use the feedback from your review to make improvements and ensure that your B-roll is high-quality and relevant. Adjust your camera settings, lighting, and shot list as needed to achieve the best results. Regular adjustments enhance the overall quality of your B-roll.

Filming B-roll in different environments requires adaptability and proper setup. Indoor and outdoor environments present unique challenges and opportunities. Adjust your equipment and settings based on the location and lighting conditions. Use appropriate accessories, such as reflectors and diffusers, to enhance your B-roll. Being adaptable ensures that you capture high-quality footage in any environment.

The role of B-roll in visual storytelling is significant. B-roll adds depth, context, and visual interest to your narrative. Use B-roll to illustrate points, provide background information, and enhance the overall storytelling experience. Thoughtful use of B-roll improves viewer engagement and retention.

Using B-roll to add depth and interest involves selecting footage that enhances your main content. B-roll can provide additional perspectives, highlight important details, and create a more immersive viewing experience. Choose clips that are relevant and add value to your narrative. Adding depth and interest with B-roll enhances the overall quality of your video.

Techniques for capturing candid B-roll include using natural movements, unobtrusive filming, and spontaneous shots. Capture real moments and interactions to add authenticity and relatability to your videos. Use techniques like long shots, reaction shots, and natural lighting to create candid and engaging B-roll. Candid footage adds a personal touch and enhances viewer connection.

Planning for B-roll during your main shoot ensures that you capture all necessary footage. Create a shot list or storyboard that includes B-roll alongside your main content. Plan your filming schedule to allow time for capturing B-roll. Proper planning ensures that you have all the footage you need to create a cohesive and engaging video.

Capturing supplemental footage enhances your main content and provides additional context. Supplemental footage includes shots that complement and support your primary narrative. Use supplemental footage to illustrate points, add variety, and create a more dynamic video. High-quality supplemental footage improves the overall production value of your content.

Techniques for handheld and stabilized shots include using tripods, gimbals, and handheld rigs. Handheld shots can add a dynamic and personal touch to your videos, while stabilized shots ensure smooth and professional footage. Use a combination of both techniques to add variety and interest to your B-roll. Proper stabilization enhances the overall quality of your video.

Reviewing B-roll for consistency ensures that your footage matches your main content. Check for consistent colors, lighting, and quality across all your B-roll clips. Make any necessary adjustments during editing to create a cohesive and professional look. Consistent B-roll enhances the overall quality and viewer experience of your video.

Editing B-roll with your main footage involves seamlessly integrating the two to create a cohesive video. Use transitions, overlays, and cuts to blend B-roll naturally with your main content. Ensure that your B-roll supports and enhances your narrative without distracting from it. Thoughtful editing of B-roll improves the overall quality of your video.

Techniques for effective B-roll use include selecting relevant footage, maintaining continuity, and using transitions. Choose B-roll clips that enhance your main content and support your narrative. Maintain continuity by matching colors, lighting, and framing. Use transitions like crossfades, dissolves, and cuts to blend B-roll seamlessly with your main footage.

Troubleshooting common B-roll issues helps address problems quickly and efficiently. Issues like shaky footage, poor lighting, and irrelevant clips can detract from your video. Use stabilization tools, adjust your lighting, and review your shot list to resolve these issues. Proper troubleshooting ensures that your B-roll is high-quality and professional.

Balancing B-roll with main footage involves finding the right mix of supplementary and primary content. Ensure that your B-roll enhances and supports your main narrative without overwhelming it. Use B-roll strategically to add variety and interest while maintaining focus on your primary message. A balanced mix of B-roll and main footage creates a cohesive and engaging video.

Keeping your B-roll organized ensures a smooth and efficient editing process. Transfer your B-roll clips to your computer and create a folder for easy access. Organize your footage into categories based on themes, scenes, or segments. Proper organization saves time and ensures that you can easily find and use your B-roll during editing.

Final tips for shooting effective B-roll include planning your shots, practicing regularly, and staying adaptable. Enjoy the process of creating and incorporating B-roll into your videos. With the right techniques and practice, you can produce high-quality B-roll that enhances your content and engages your audience.

Chapter 21: Shoot Your Thumbnail

———

The importance of a compelling thumbnail cannot be overstated. Thumbnails serve as the visual representation of your video and play a crucial role in attracting viewers. A well-designed thumbnail grabs attention, conveys the essence of your content, and encourages viewers to click on your video. Investing time and effort into creating a captivating thumbnail is essential for increasing your video's click-through rate.

Planning your thumbnail concept involves thinking about what elements will grab attention and accurately represent your content. Consider using bold colors, clear images, and concise text to create an engaging and visually appealing thumbnail. A strong concept sets the foundation for a successful thumbnail.

Techniques for capturing an eye-catching thumbnail include using high-quality images, clear focal points, and dynamic compositions. Use a camera or phone with a high-resolution camera to capture sharp and clear images. Focus on a single subject or element to create a clear focal point. Experiment with different compositions to add interest and variety.

Using text effectively in your thumbnail helps convey important information and enhances viewer engagement. Use bold and readable fonts to add titles, captions, or keywords to your thumbnail. Keep the text concise and relevant to the content. Effective use of text adds context and encourages viewers to click on your video.

Balancing colors and contrast is crucial for creating a visually appealing thumbnail. Use complementary colors to make your thumbnail stand out and attract attention. Adjust the contrast to ensure that your images and text are clear and easy to read. Balanced colors and contrast enhance the overall quality of your thumbnail.

The role of facial expressions and emotions in thumbnails is significant. Thumbnails with expressive faces and emotions create a personal connection and draw viewers in. Use clear and exaggerated facial expressions to convey emotions and capture attention. Emotionally engaging thumbnails encourage viewers to click on your video.

Using close-ups and clear images enhances the visual impact of your thumbnail. Close-up shots create a strong focal point and highlight important details. Ensure that your images are sharp and clear to maintain visual quality. High-quality close-ups make your thumbnail more engaging and professional.

Capturing different poses and angles provides variety and interest in your thumbnails. Experiment with various poses, expressions, and angles to create dynamic and engaging thumbnails. Use a tripod or stabilizer to keep your shots steady and professional. Different poses and angles add variety and visual interest to your thumbnails.

Techniques for editing and enhancing your thumbnail include using photo editing software to adjust colors, brightness, and contrast. Use tools like Adobe Photoshop, Canva, or PicMonkey to enhance your images and add text. Editing ensures that your thumbnail is polished and professional. Regularly review and refine your editing techniques to achieve the best results.

Using overlays and effects adds visual interest and highlights important elements in your thumbnail. Use overlays like shapes, lines, and graphics to draw attention to key points. Effects like shadows, glows, and gradients add depth and dimension. Thoughtful use of overlays and effects enhances the overall quality of your thumbnail.

Reviewing and selecting the best thumbnail involves comparing different options and choosing the most engaging and relevant one. Review your captured images and edited thumbnails to identify the strongest option. Consider factors like clarity, visual appeal, and relevance to the content. Selecting the best thumbnail ensures that your video attracts attention and encourages clicks.

Testing different thumbnail designs provides insights into what resonates with your audience. Experiment with various styles, colors, and compositions to see what works best. Use A/B testing to compare the performance of different thumbnails and make data-driven decisions. Regular testing and refinement improve your thumbnail design skills and engagement.

Incorporating branding elements into your thumbnail strengthens your brand identity. Use consistent colors, fonts, and logos to create a cohesive look. Branding elements make your thumbnails more recognizable and reinforce your brand. Consistent branding enhances viewer recognition and trust.

Using thumbnails to set viewer expectations involves accurately representing your content. Ensure that your thumbnail aligns with the video's theme and message. Misleading thumbnails can lead to viewer dissatisfaction and lower engagement. Accurate and honest thumbnails build trust and encourage viewer retention.

The impact of thumbnails on click-through rate cannot be overstated. A compelling thumbnail significantly increases the likelihood that viewers will click on your video. Invest time and effort into creating engaging and visually appealing thumbnails to boost your click-through rate and overall video performance.

Creating custom thumbnails for different platforms ensures that your content stands out across various channels. Different platforms have unique requirements and audience preferences. Customize your thumbnails for YouTube, social media, and other platforms to maximize their effectiveness. Custom thumbnails enhance your overall reach and engagement.

Tips for avoiding common thumbnail mistakes include avoiding clutter, using clear images, and maintaining consistency. Cluttered thumbnails can be overwhelming and distracting. Use clear and high-quality images to create a clean and professional look. Maintain consistency in your design to reinforce your brand. Avoiding these mistakes ensures that your thumbnails are effective and engaging.

Balancing simplicity and creativity in your thumbnails involves using clear and engaging designs. While it's important to be creative, avoid overcomplicating your thumbnails. Focus on creating a strong focal point and clear message. Simple and creative thumbnails are visually appealing and effective.

The importance of regularly updating your thumbnail skills cannot be overstated. Stay updated with design trends, tools, and techniques to keep your thumbnails fresh and engaging. Regularly review and refine your skills to stay competitive and relevant. Continuous improvement ensures that your thumbnails remain high-quality and effective.

Using analytics to refine your thumbnail strategy provides valuable insights into what works best for your audience. Track the performance of your thumbnails using YouTube Analytics and other tools. Use this data to make informed decisions and improve your thumbnail design. Analytics help you understand viewer preferences and enhance your overall strategy.

Collaborating with designers for professional thumbnails can elevate your content. If you're not confident in your design skills, consider working with a professional designer. Platforms like Fiverr and Upwork connect you with talented designers who can create custom thumbnails. Professional thumbnails enhance your brand and overall video quality.

The role of thumbnails in overall video performance is significant. Thumbnails are often the first impression viewers have of your content. A compelling and visually appealing thumbnail attracts attention and encourages clicks. Investing in high-quality thumbnails improves your video's performance and viewer engagement.

Final tips for creating compelling thumbnails include staying creative, practicing regularly, and using feedback to improve. Enjoy the process of designing and refining your thumbnails. With the right techniques and practice, you can create engaging and visually appealing thumbnails that captivate your audience.

Chapter 22: Edit Your Footage

———

The importance of editing in video production cannot be overstated. Editing transforms raw footage into a polished and professional video. It allows you to refine your content, enhance visual and audio quality, and create a cohesive narrative. Effective editing ensures that your videos are engaging, clear, and aligned with your goals.

Choosing the right editing software for your needs is the first step. There are various options available, ranging from beginner-friendly tools to professional-grade software. Popular choices include Adobe Premiere Pro, Final Cut Pro, DaVinci Resolve, and iMovie. Select software that matches your skill level and editing requirements. Investing in the right tools ensures that you can achieve high-quality results.

Organizing your footage and assets before editing streamlines the process and saves time. Create folders for your video clips, audio files, graphics, and other elements. Label and sort your assets based on scenes, themes, or segments. Proper organization ensures that you can easily access and use your materials during editing.

Importing and arranging your clips is the next step. Import your footage and assets into your editing software and arrange them on the timeline. Start with your main footage and add supplementary clips, such as B-roll, cutaways, and transitions. Arranging your clips provides a clear structure for your video and sets the foundation for editing.

Techniques for trimming and cutting your footage involve removing unnecessary parts and refining your content. Use tools like the razor tool and ripple edit to cut and trim your clips. Focus on maintaining a smooth and cohesive flow. Trimming and cutting ensure that your video is concise, engaging, and free from distractions.

Adding transitions and effects enhances the visual appeal and continuity of your video. Use transitions like fades, dissolves, and cuts to connect different segments smoothly. Apply effects like color correction, stabilization, and overlays to enhance visual quality. Thoughtful use of transitions and effects adds a professional touch to your video.

Syncing audio with your video footage is crucial for a seamless viewing experience. Align your audio tracks with the corresponding video clips using sync points or waveforms. Adjust the timing to ensure that your audio matches the video perfectly. Proper synchronization ensures that your audio and video are cohesive and engaging.

Enhancing audio quality involves using tools like noise reduction, equalization, and compression. Remove background noise, adjust volume levels, and balance your audio tracks. Use audio effects to enhance clarity and add depth. High-quality audio enhances the overall viewer experience and engagement.

Using color correction and grading improves the visual quality and consistency of your video. Adjust the brightness, contrast, saturation, and white balance to achieve the desired look. Apply color grading to create a specific mood or style. Proper color correction and grading ensure that your video is visually appealing and professional.

Incorporating graphics and text adds context and visual interest to your video. Use titles, captions, lower thirds, and overlays to highlight important information and enhance viewer understanding. Choose fonts, colors, and styles that match your brand and content. Thoughtful use of graphics and text improves engagement and clarity.

Adding background music and sound effects enhances the overall mood and engagement of your video. Choose royalty-free music and sound effects that complement your content and create the desired atmosphere. Adjust the volume levels to balance the audio tracks. Background music and sound effects add depth and interest to your video.

Techniques for smooth transitions between clips include using crossfades, dissolves, and cuts. Transitions help create a seamless flow and maintain viewer engagement. Use transitions thoughtfully to enhance the narrative and avoid jarring cuts. Smooth transitions improve the overall quality of your video.

Creating a cohesive narrative involves arranging your clips and audio to tell a clear and engaging story. Focus on the structure, pacing, and flow of your video. Ensure that each segment supports the overall message and contributes to the narrative. A cohesive narrative keeps viewers interested and engaged.

Reviewing and refining your edit helps identify areas for improvement. Watch your edited video multiple times and look for any issues or inconsistencies. Make necessary adjustments to improve clarity, flow, and engagement. Regular review and refinement ensure that your final video is high-quality and professional.

Exporting your video involves choosing the right settings and format for your platform. Select the appropriate resolution, frame rate, and compression settings based on your needs. Common formats include MP4, MOV, and AVI. Proper exporting ensures that your video maintains its quality and is compatible with your chosen platform.

Using templates and presets can streamline the editing process and ensure consistency. Many editing software programs offer templates and presets for transitions, effects, and color grading. Use these resources to save time and maintain a professional look. Templates and presets provide a starting point for customization and refinement.

Techniques for adding visual and audio effects include using filters, overlays, and plugins. Visual effects enhance the visual appeal, while audio effects improve sound quality and add interest. Experiment with different effects to achieve the desired look and feel. Thoughtful use of effects enhances the overall quality of your video.

Managing storage and file formats is essential for efficient editing and archiving. Use high-capacity storage devices and cloud services to store your footage and project files. Choose file formats that balance quality and storage efficiency. Regularly back up your files to prevent data loss. Proper storage management ensures that your editing process is smooth and organized.

Using keyboard shortcuts and workflow techniques can speed up the editing process. Learn and use shortcuts for common tasks like cutting, trimming, and adding effects. Develop a workflow that includes organizing, importing, editing, and exporting. Efficient editing techniques save time and improve productivity.

Collaborating with others during editing involves sharing project files and receiving feedback. Use cloud services and collaboration tools to share your work with team members or clients. Incorporate their feedback to refine and improve your edit. Collaboration enhances creativity and ensures that your final video meets your goals.

Troubleshooting common editing issues helps address problems quickly and efficiently. Issues like crashes, glitches, and audio sync problems can be frustrating. Learn basic troubleshooting techniques to resolve these issues on the spot. Being prepared ensures that you can handle any challenges during editing.

Using analytics to refine your editing process provides valuable insights into viewer preferences. Track the performance of your videos using YouTube Analytics and other tools. Use this data to identify what works and what needs improvement. Analytics help you make informed decisions and enhance your overall strategy.

Final tips for effective video editing include staying organized, practicing regularly, and being adaptable. Enjoy the process of creating and refining your videos. With the right techniques and practice, you can produce high-quality, engaging, and professional videos that captivate your audience.

Chapter 23: Upload Your First Video

Uploading your first video to YouTube is an exciting milestone in your journey as a creator. The importance of a successful upload cannot be overstated, as it sets the stage for your channel's growth and viewer engagement. Properly preparing your video for upload ensures that it reaches and resonates with your audience.

Choosing the right video title is the first step in the upload process. Your title should be clear, concise, and relevant to your content. Use keywords that accurately describe your video and make it easy for viewers to find. A compelling title grabs attention and encourages clicks.

Writing an engaging video description helps provide context and additional information about your content. Include a brief summary of your video, relevant keywords, and links to your social media profiles, website, or other resources. An informative and well-structured description enhances viewer understanding and engagement.

Using tags and keywords effectively improves your video's discoverability on YouTube. Choose relevant and specific tags that describe your content and align with your target audience's search terms. Keywords help YouTube's algorithm understand and categorize your video, increasing its visibility.

Creating a custom thumbnail is essential for attracting viewers and increasing click-through rates. Design a visually appealing and relevant thumbnail that accurately represents your content. Use high-quality images, bold colors, and clear text to create an eye-catching thumbnail. A compelling thumbnail enhances the overall appeal of your video.

Setting video visibility and privacy options involves choosing whether your video will be public, private, or unlisted. Public videos are visible to everyone, private videos are only accessible to you, and unlisted videos can be shared via a direct link. Choose the option that best suits your goals and audience.

Scheduling your video for optimal release times helps maximize viewer engagement. Research your target audience's viewing habits and choose a time when they are most likely to watch. Scheduling your video for peak times increases visibility and engagement. Consistent scheduling also helps build viewer anticipation and loyalty.

Adding video cards and end screens provides additional opportunities for viewer engagement. Video cards are interactive elements that link to other videos, playlists, or external sites. End screens appear at the end of your video and promote related content or encourage actions like subscribing. Use these tools to enhance viewer interaction and retention.

Using YouTube's advanced settings allows you to customize your video's settings and optimize its performance. Adjust options like comments, captions, and monetization to suit your needs. Advanced settings provide more control over your video's presentation and engagement.

Engaging with your audience through comments and interactions helps build a loyal community. Respond to comments, answer questions, and acknowledge viewer feedback. Active engagement shows that you value your audience and fosters a sense of connection. Building a community enhances viewer loyalty and retention.

Promoting your video on social media and other platforms increases its reach and visibility. Share your video on Facebook, Twitter, Instagram, and other social media channels. Use relevant hashtags, tags, and captions to attract viewers. Cross-promotion helps you reach a broader audience and drive traffic to your video.

Using YouTube Analytics to track your video's performance provides valuable insights. Monitor metrics like views, watch time, audience demographics, and engagement rates. Use this data to understand how your video is performing and identify areas for improvement. Analytics help you make informed decisions and optimize your content strategy.

Updating your video based on feedback and performance data ensures that it remains relevant and engaging. Use viewer comments and analytics to identify what resonates with your audience and what needs adjustment. Regularly updating your video enhances its performance and viewer satisfaction.

The role of SEO in video discoverability is significant. Optimize your video's title, description, tags, and keywords for search engines. Use relevant and specific terms that align with your target audience's search queries. SEO helps your video rank higher in search results and attract more viewers.

Creating playlists and organizing your videos helps improve viewer navigation and engagement. Group related videos into playlists based on themes, topics, or series. Playlists encourage viewers to watch multiple videos and stay engaged with your content. Proper organization enhances the overall viewer experience.

Using YouTube's promotional tools, such as ads and collaborations, can boost your video's visibility. Consider running YouTube ads to reach a broader audience and increase views. Collaborate with other creators to cross-promote your content and attract new viewers. Promotional tools help you grow your channel and enhance your reach.

The importance of a strong call to action cannot be overstated. Encourage viewers to like, comment, subscribe, and share your video. A clear and compelling call to action motivates viewers to engage with your content and support your channel. Effective calls to action enhance viewer interaction and retention.

Reviewing and refining your upload process ensures that you consistently produce high-quality videos. Regularly assess your upload strategy, settings, and engagement techniques. Make necessary adjustments to improve your video's performance and viewer satisfaction. Continuous refinement ensures that your channel remains relevant and successful.

The impact of video thumbnails on click-through rate is significant. A well-designed thumbnail attracts attention and encourages viewers to click on your video. Invest time and effort into creating engaging and visually appealing thumbnails. High-quality thumbnails improve your video's performance and overall engagement.

Using YouTube's community features, such as posts and stories, enhances viewer interaction. Community posts allow you to share updates, polls, and images with your audience. Stories provide short, engaging clips that promote your content and engage viewers. Using these features fosters a sense of community and enhances viewer loyalty.

Balancing promotion and engagement involves effectively promoting your video while maintaining active viewer interaction. Share your video across various platforms and engage with your audience through comments and interactions. A balanced approach ensures that your video reaches a broad audience and builds a loyal community.

Final tips for a successful video upload include staying organized, optimizing your settings, and actively engaging with your audience. Enjoy the process of sharing your content and connecting with your viewers. With the right techniques and practice, you can achieve successful uploads and grow your YouTube channel.

Chapter 24: Promote Your Video

———

Promoting your video effectively is crucial for increasing visibility, engagement, and channel growth. The importance of promotion cannot be overstated, as it helps you reach a broader audience and drive traffic to your content. Proper promotion ensures that your video is seen by the right viewers and achieves its intended goals.

Using social media platforms to share your video increases its reach and visibility. Share your video on Facebook, Twitter, Instagram, and other social media channels. Use relevant hashtags, tags, and captions to attract viewers and encourage engagement. Social media promotion helps you reach a wider audience and drive traffic to your video.

Engaging with online communities and forums allows you to connect with potential viewers who are interested in your content. Participate in discussions, share your video, and provide valuable insights related to your niche. Engaging with online communities builds awareness and drives traffic to your video.

Collaborating with other YouTubers and influencers can significantly boost your video's visibility. Partner with creators who share a similar audience or niche. Collaborations introduce your channel to new viewers and provide valuable networking opportunities. Cross-promotion with other creators enhances your reach and engagement.

Using email marketing to promote your video helps you reach your existing audience directly. Send newsletters or updates to your email subscribers with a link to your video. Provide a brief summary and compelling reasons for them to watch. Email marketing ensures that your loyal followers stay informed and engaged with your content.

Creating teaser clips and previews provides a sneak peek of your video and generates interest. Share short clips or highlights on social media and other platforms to attract viewers. Teasers create anticipation and encourage viewers to watch the full video. Properly edited previews enhance viewer curiosity and engagement.

Optimizing your video for SEO improves its discoverability on YouTube and search engines. Use relevant keywords in your title, description, and tags. Write a detailed and informative description that includes key terms related to your content. SEO optimization helps your video rank higher in search results and attract more viewers.

Using YouTube's promotional tools, such as ads and cards, can boost your video's visibility. Consider running YouTube ads to reach a broader audience and increase views. Use video cards to promote related content, playlists, or external links. Promotional tools help you grow your channel and enhance your reach.

Engaging with your audience through comments and interactions builds a loyal community. Respond to comments, answer questions, and acknowledge viewer feedback. Active engagement shows that you value your audience and fosters a sense of connection. Building a community enhances viewer loyalty and retention.

Hosting contests and giveaways encourages viewer participation and engagement. Create contests that require viewers to watch, like, comment, or share your video. Offer attractive prizes to motivate participation. Contests and giveaways increase viewer interaction and drive traffic to your video.

Using analytics to track your video's performance provides valuable insights. Monitor metrics like views, watch time, audience demographics, and engagement rates. Use this data to understand how your video is performing and identify areas for improvement. Analytics help you make informed decisions and optimize your promotion strategy.

Creating playlists and organizing your videos improves viewer navigation and engagement. Group related videos into playlists based on themes, topics, or series. Playlists encourage viewers to watch multiple videos and stay engaged with your content. Proper organization enhances the overall viewer experience.

Using hashtags and tags effectively increases your video's discoverability on social media and YouTube. Choose relevant and specific tags that describe your content and align with your target audience's search terms. Hashtags and tags help your video reach a broader audience and attract more viewers.

Cross-promoting your video on your blog or website drives traffic to your content. Embed your video in blog posts or create dedicated pages to promote it. Write a brief summary or article related to the video to provide additional context. Cross-promotion enhances your overall reach and engagement.

Collaborating with brands and sponsors can provide valuable exposure and support. Partner with brands that align with your content and audience. Sponsored content introduces your channel to new viewers and provides additional resources for promotion. Brand collaborations enhance your reach and credibility.

Using live streams and events to promote your video creates real-time engagement. Host live streams to discuss your video, answer questions, and interact with your audience. Promote your video during the live stream to drive traffic and engagement. Live events provide a unique opportunity to connect with your viewers.

Promoting your video through paid advertising increases its visibility and reach. Use platforms like Google Ads, Facebook Ads, and Instagram Ads to run targeted campaigns. Set a budget, define your target audience, and create compelling ads to attract viewers. Paid advertising enhances your promotion efforts and drives traffic to your video.

Networking with other creators and industry professionals provides valuable opportunities for collaboration and promotion. Attend industry events, participate in online groups, and connect with fellow creators. Networking helps you build relationships and expand your reach. Collaborations and partnerships enhance your overall promotion strategy.

The importance of consistent promotion cannot be overstated. Regularly promote your video across various platforms and engage with your audience.

Consistency builds awareness and encourages viewer loyalty. A sustained promotion effort ensures that your video reaches its full potential.

Using storytelling and compelling narratives in your promotion materials attracts viewers and generates interest. Share the story behind your video, your creative process, or personal experiences related to the content. Storytelling adds a personal touch and engages viewers on a deeper level.

Final tips for effective video promotion include staying organized, being creative, and actively engaging with your audience. Enjoy the process of sharing and promoting your content. With the right techniques and practice, you can achieve successful promotion and grow your YouTube channel.

Chapter 25: Consistency is Key

The importance of consistency in video production cannot be overstated. Consistent uploads and engagement help build a loyal audience, improve your channel's visibility, and enhance viewer retention. Regularly producing and sharing high-quality content ensures that your viewers stay engaged and return for more.

Developing a content schedule helps you plan and organize your video production. Create a calendar that outlines your upload dates, content themes, and promotional activities. A content schedule provides structure and ensures that you consistently produce and share new videos. Planning ahead enhances your productivity and content quality.

Setting realistic goals and expectations is crucial for maintaining consistency. Define your short-term and long-term objectives, such as upload frequency, subscriber growth, and engagement rates. Set achievable milestones that motivate you to stay on track. Realistic goals ensure that you remain focused and committed to your channel.

The role of planning and preparation in consistency is significant. Proper planning involves brainstorming video ideas, writing scripts, and organizing your filming schedule. Preparation includes setting up your equipment, testing your setup, and rehearsing your delivery. Planning and preparation ensure that your content is well-structured and high-quality.

Techniques for staying motivated and productive include setting deadlines, celebrating milestones, and taking breaks when needed. Deadlines provide a sense of urgency and keep you accountable. Celebrating achievements, no matter how small, boosts your motivation and morale. Taking breaks helps prevent burnout and maintains your creativity.

Using analytics to track your progress provides valuable insights into your channel's performance. Monitor metrics like views, watch time, audience demographics, and engagement rates. Use this data to understand what's working and what needs improvement. Analytics help you make informed decisions and optimize your content strategy.

The impact of consistency on viewer loyalty and retention is significant. Regular uploads and engagement build trust and familiarity with your audience. Consistency signals that you are committed to providing valuable content, encouraging viewers to subscribe and return for more. Loyal viewers enhance your channel's growth and success.

Creating a content backlog ensures that you always have videos ready for upload. Film and edit multiple videos in advance to maintain a steady upload schedule. A content backlog provides a buffer for unexpected delays or busy periods. Proper planning and preparation ensure that you consistently produce and share new videos.

Engaging with your audience regularly helps build a strong and loyal community. Respond to comments, ask for feedback, and create content that addresses viewer interests and concerns. Active engagement shows that you value your audience and fosters a sense of connection. Building a community enhances viewer loyalty and retention.

Using collaboration and networking to maintain consistency provides support and inspiration. Partner with other creators to share ideas, resources, and audience. Collaborations introduce your channel to new viewers and provide valuable networking opportunities. Regular networking enhances your creativity and consistency.

The role of adaptability and flexibility in maintaining consistency is significant. Be prepared to adjust your content, schedule, and strategy based on feedback and performance data. Adaptability ensures that you remain relevant and responsive to your audience's needs. Flexibility enhances your overall content quality and viewer engagement.

Tips for managing time effectively include prioritizing tasks, setting deadlines, and using productivity tools. Focus on the most important and time-sensitive tasks first. Set deadlines for each stage of your video production process. Use productivity tools like calendars, to-do lists, and project management apps to stay organized and efficient.

Balancing quality and quantity is crucial for maintaining consistency. While it's important to produce high-quality content, avoid sacrificing quantity for perfection. Find a balance that allows you to regularly upload engaging and professional videos. Consistent quality enhances viewer satisfaction and retention.

Creating a content calendar helps you plan and organize your video production. Outline your upload dates, content themes, and promotional activities. A content calendar provides structure and ensures that you consistently produce and share new videos. Planning ahead enhances your productivity and content quality.

Using batch filming and editing techniques streamlines your production process. Film multiple videos in one session to save time and effort. Batch editing allows you to focus on one task at a time, increasing efficiency. These techniques ensure that you have a steady stream of content ready for upload.

The importance of setting boundaries and managing expectations cannot be overstated. Avoid overcommitting or setting unrealistic goals that can lead to burnout. Set clear boundaries for your work and personal life to maintain a healthy balance. Managing expectations ensures that you remain motivated and productive.

Using templates and presets for editing and graphics saves time and ensures consistency. Many editing software programs offer templates and presets for transitions, effects, and color grading. Use these resources to maintain a professional and cohesive look. Templates and presets provide a starting point for customization and refinement.

Incorporating viewer feedback into your content strategy helps you stay relevant and responsive. Pay attention to comments, messages, and engagement metrics to understand what resonates with your audience. Use this feedback to shape your content and improve your strategy. Regularly updating your approach enhances viewer satisfaction and retention.

Tips for avoiding burnout include taking breaks, setting boundaries, and seeking support. Regular breaks help you recharge and maintain creativity. Set clear boundaries for your work and personal life to prevent overcommitting. Seek support from friends, family, or fellow creators to stay motivated and inspired.

The impact of consistent branding on viewer recognition and loyalty is significant. Use consistent colors, fonts, logos, and design elements across your videos and promotional materials. Consistent branding reinforces your identity and makes your content more recognizable. Branding consistency enhances viewer loyalty and trust.

Using automation tools for scheduling and promoting your videos saves time and effort. Tools like Hootsuite, Buffer, and TubeBuddy allow you to schedule uploads, social media posts, and promotional activities in advance. Automation ensures that your content is consistently shared and promoted, enhancing your reach and engagement.

Final tips for maintaining consistency include staying organized, setting realistic goals, and actively engaging with your audience. Enjoy the process of creating and sharing your content. With the right techniques and practice, you can achieve consistency and grow your YouTube channel.

Chapter 26: Optimize for SEO

The importance of SEO (Search Engine Optimization) in video production cannot be overstated. SEO helps improve your video's visibility on YouTube and search engines, increasing its chances of being discovered by viewers. Proper SEO ensures that your content reaches a broader audience and achieves its intended goals.

Understanding keywords and their role in SEO is the first step. Keywords are terms and phrases that describe your content and match what viewers are searching for. Use keyword research tools like Google Keyword Planner, Ahrefs, and TubeBuddy to identify relevant and high-traffic keywords. Choosing the right keywords ensures that your video ranks higher in search results.

Optimizing your video title involves incorporating relevant keywords while keeping it clear and engaging. Your title should accurately describe your content and attract viewers' attention. Use primary keywords at the beginning of your title for better visibility. A well-optimized title enhances your video's discoverability and click-through rate.

Writing an informative and keyword-rich video description helps improve SEO and provide context for viewers. Include a detailed summary of your video, relevant keywords, and links to your social media profiles, website, or other resources. Use natural language and avoid keyword stuffing. An optimized description enhances your video's searchability and viewer engagement.

Using tags effectively involves selecting relevant and specific tags that describe your content. Tags help YouTube's algorithm understand and categorize your video, increasing its visibility. Use a mix of broad and specific tags to cover different aspects of your content. Effective tagging improves your video's discoverability and reach.

Creating engaging and relevant thumbnails attracts viewers and improves click-through rates. Design a visually appealing thumbnail that accurately represents your content. Use high-quality images, bold colors, and clear text to create an eye-catching thumbnail. A compelling thumbnail enhances the overall appeal of your video.

Optimizing video transcripts and captions improves accessibility and SEO. Transcripts provide text versions of your video's audio, making it easier for search engines to index your content. Use captions to improve accessibility for viewers with hearing impairments. Properly optimized transcripts and captions enhance your video's searchability and viewer engagement.

Using video cards and end screens to promote related content and encourage viewer interaction improves SEO. Video cards are interactive elements that link to other videos, playlists, or external sites. End screens appear at the end of your video and promote related content or encourage actions like subscribing. These tools enhance viewer retention and engagement.

Creating playlists and organizing your videos improves viewer navigation and engagement. Group related videos into playlists based on themes, topics, or series. Playlists encourage viewers to watch multiple videos and stay engaged with your content. Proper organization enhances the overall viewer experience.

Using YouTube's advanced settings to optimize your video's performance involves adjusting options like comments, captions, and monetization. Enable comments to encourage viewer interaction and engagement. Use captions to improve accessibility and SEO. Advanced settings provide more control over your video's presentation and engagement.

Promoting your video on social media and other platforms increases its reach and visibility. Share your video on Facebook, Twitter, Instagram, and other social media channels. Use relevant hashtags, tags, and captions to attract viewers. Cross-promotion helps you reach a broader audience and drive traffic to your video.

Engaging with your audience through comments and interactions builds a loyal community and improves SEO. Respond to comments, answer questions, and acknowledge viewer feedback. Active engagement shows that you value your audience and fosters a sense of connection. Building a community enhances viewer loyalty and retention.

Using analytics to track your video's performance provides valuable insights. Monitor metrics like views, watch time, audience demographics, and engagement rates. Use this data to understand how your video is performing and identify areas for improvement. Analytics help you make informed decisions and optimize your content strategy.

Optimizing your channel for SEO involves using keywords, tags, and descriptions to improve discoverability. Include relevant keywords in your channel name, description, and tags. Use a clear and engaging description that outlines your content and goals. Properly optimized channels rank higher in search results and attract more viewers.

Using collaborations and guest appearances to enhance SEO introduces your channel to new audiences and provides valuable backlinks. Partner with other creators to share ideas, resources, and audience. Collaborations introduce your channel to new viewers and provide valuable networking opportunities. Cross-promotion with other creators enhances your reach and engagement.

Creating content that answers viewer questions and addresses their needs improves SEO. Focus on providing valuable and informative content that resonates with your target audience. Use keywords and phrases that match what viewers are searching for. Relevant and high-quality content improves your video's ranking and viewer engagement.

Using backlinks and external links to promote your video enhances SEO. Include links to your video on your website, blog, and social media profiles. Backlinks from reputable sources improve your video's credibility and search ranking. Proper link-building strategies enhance your video's discoverability and reach.

The importance of mobile optimization cannot be overstated. Ensure that your video is optimized for mobile devices, as a significant portion of viewers access YouTube on their phones. Use responsive design, clear text, and high-quality images to create a mobile-friendly experience. Mobile optimization enhances viewer engagement and retention.

Creating a strong call to action encourages viewers to like, comment, subscribe, and share your video. A clear and compelling call to action motivates viewers to engage with your content and support your channel. Effective calls to action enhance viewer interaction and retention.

Using analytics to refine your SEO strategy provides valuable insights into viewer preferences and behavior. Track the performance of your videos using YouTube Analytics and other tools. Use this data to identify what works and what needs improvement. Analytics help you make informed decisions and enhance your overall SEO strategy.

Regularly updating your content and SEO practices ensures that your videos remain relevant and discoverable. Stay updated with the latest SEO trends, tools, and techniques. Regularly review and refine your keywords, tags, and descriptions to maintain optimal performance. Continuous improvement ensures that your videos stay competitive and successful.

The impact of SEO on overall channel growth is significant. Properly optimized videos attract more viewers, improve engagement, and enhance viewer retention. Invest time and effort into understanding and implementing effective SEO practices. SEO optimization ensures that your channel reaches its full potential and achieves its goals.

Final tips for optimizing your videos for SEO include staying organized, using relevant keywords, and actively engaging with your audience. Enjoy the process of creating and sharing your content. With the right techniques and practice, you can achieve successful SEO optimization and grow your YouTube channel.

www.ingramcontent.com/pod-product-compliance
Lightning Source LLC
LaVergne TN
LVHW051742050326
832903LV00029B/2678